the SUPER simple guide to CORALS

James Fatherree

T.F.H. Publications, Inc.

I would like to give large and special thanks to aquarists Eric Borneman, Charles Delbeek, Bob Fenner, Bob Goemans, Martin Moe, Ron Shimek, Julian Sprung, and Nancy Stone for their various influences on my life. Without all of them, it would be different in countless unknown ways, and while there's always room for improvement, I happen to like it quite a lot the way it is.

JWF

T.F.H. Publications, Inc.
One TFH Plaza
Third and Union Avenues
Neptune City, NJ 07753

Library of Congress Cataloging-in-Publication Data
Fatherree, Jim.
The super simple guide to corals / James Fatherree.
p. cm.
Includes index.
ISBN 0-7938-3456-2 (alk. paper)
1. Corals. I. Title.
SF458.C64F29 2004
639.7--dc22
2004002528

All Photographs by James Fatherree

Cartoons by Michael Pifer

www.tfh.com

Contents

Start
Your Own
Colonies!

Part Four: Guide to Common Corals 69

Coral
Requirements

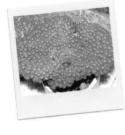

Part One
Coral Biology

"Symbiotic relationship my foot! Every time I swim through that thing, someone steals my wallet!

Introduction

So you want to keep live corals in an aquarium, huh? While keeping aquariums has been a beloved pastime for millions of people around the world for decades, the idea of being able to successfully keep live corals in reef aquariums has only become popular in the last few years. Over this relatively short period of time, the coral-

Creating beautiful reef aquariums takes time and patience.

keeping hobby has literally exploded, and now you can be a part of it, too. It takes patience, though, and it is essential that you do a good bit of homework as well.

While the amount of information required to be a successful "reefer" is substantial and oftentimes presented in language that's hard to digest, I've done what I can to make things as *super simple* as possible. The basics are all here, and by the time you're done with this book, you should have a greater understanding of various coral animals that will help you get off to a great start. We'll look at how they "work," what it takes to keep them happy and healthy, which corals are compatible with each other, and proper placement of the corals in the aquarium. We'll even go over various ways that you can multiply the number of corals you have, pick the best specimens in the shop, and many other topics.

Enjoy, and good luck in your coral-keeping ventures!

Natural History of Cnidarians

Biologists split up and sort out organisms into large groupings called phyla, and all of the members of one phylum are distinct from all of those in other phyla based on various unique features. For example, while they may look and act very differently, a shrimp and a spider are both placed together in the phylum

Cnidarians come in many forms, but they all share some features.

Arthropoda because they both have an exoskeleton and jointed appendages. Other animals that have these same features are also lumped together with them, while anything that doesn't have them must belong to some other phylum. As you'll see, overall appearance or lifestyle doesn't matter at all when it comes to placement, as long as particular given features are shared. This is especially true of the more than 9,000 members of the phylum Cnidaria (pronounced ny-dare-e-ah as the "c" is silent), which includes the jellyfishes, sea anemones, and corals.

Common Traits

There are several things these animals have in common, the first of which is a body formed by a simple outer layer and an inner layer of tissue. On the outside, they are covered by the ectodermis,

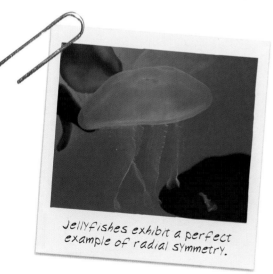

Jellyfishes exhibit a perfect example of radial symmetry.

which acts like the animal's skin. The endodermis, found on the inside and also referred to as the gastrodermis, forms a mouth and a stomach. A soft, jelly-like material called the mesoglea exists as a layer in between the two. A number of simple filamentous muscles and a few nerves also run throughout these layers, but not much more does. Overall, cnidarians are some of the simplest multi-celled organisms around.

Another key characteristic of cnidarians is a body plan that is radial by design, with parts located around a central axis. This is called radial symmetry, and it means that in some way, they can be divided up into radial sections that are mirror images of each other. Just think of a jellyfish, for example. You could cut one into countless pie-shaped slices, and all of them would look essentially the same. By comparison, humans have bilateral symmetry and could be split down the middle into only two sections that are mirror images: the left and right halves. One thing to keep in mind, though, is that radial symmetry is sometimes lost as cnidarians age or form various sorts of colonies, and thus may only be seen when they are young.

A mouth that opens up into the pouch formed by the endodermis (which acts as the stomach), is located at the hub of a cnidarian's body. This digestive structure, called the enteron or gastrovascular cavity, really can't be considered a digestive "system," though, because there aren't any intestines or other such related structures. Instead, the mouth also acts as the exit for any wastes and undigested material.

These colonial polyps clearly reveal a mouth surrounded by a ring of tentacles used for food capture.

Despite their appearence, upside-down jellies are not a link between sessile corals and jellyfishes.

The mouth is typically able to open up surprisingly wide and is surrounded by a ring of tentacles of some size. Their function is to help capture and ingest food (although you'll see later that there are exceptions). Also, these tentacles are covered by cnidocytes, thousands of specialized stinging and/or adhesive cells that aid in food capture. Tentacles are unique to the members of this phylum as well.

While all cnidarians possess the features covered above, they can all still be subdivided on the basis of finer structural details and a few other factors. For example, corals don't swim, but jellyfishes do. As a result, even though they are all radial, symmetrical, and have cnidocytes, etc., jellies and corals are placed in separate subgroups within the phylum. Likewise, hydras and fire corals (which aren't really corals) are separated from the others as well. With that said, understand that "corals" are actually numerous types of animals within the phylum Cnidaria, all of which share some common features that the other animals don't. All corals are placed into a subgroup of the phylum called the class Anthozoa.

Basic Coral Anatomy

Individual coral animals are called "polyps." They can live a solitary existence as a single polyp, or they can live in various colonies made up of numerous polyps in which individuals aren't so individual anymore and may not be recognizable at first glance. However, while this is the case for the untrained eye, if you look at

Polyps often extend some distance from the coral's skeleton.

enough of them and understand what polyps are, they become quite obvious regardless of how they are arranged and packaged.

The typical single polyp has its own centrally located mouth and gastrovascular cavity with a ring of tentacles circling them. The tentacles may vary in form from long, thin, and smooth to short and pinnate (with pinnate meaning the tentacles have small side projections that make them look almost like feathers). However, the overall body plan of each polyp in colonies is typically the same too, as each has a body, mouth, gastrovascular cavity, and tentacles.

There are deviations, though, due to the fact that there are some corals that have very small tentacles or even lack them altogether, but these are the minority. Likewise, there are some soft-bodied corals that may have trunks and/or branches that lack "ordinary" polyps on much of their surfaces. However, at least a few will be visible somewhere on their tops or on the ends of their branches.

Skeletal Structure

In addition to many types of soft-bodied corals, there are a vast number of stony/hard corals that produce skeletons. These corals take calcium from seawater and combine it with carbon dioxide to form calcium carbonate, which is a white-colored solid called "aragonite." It is also often called "limestone" because limestone rocks are composed of calcium carbonate as well.

Part 1

Solitary stony corals may have a skeleton that is completely internal, like your bones, but many also have skeletons that are partially exposed, with the coral only covering the upper portions of the outer surface. Think of a solitary stony coral as a jellyfish turned upside down in a bowl, with some of the flesh wrapping over the rim of the bowl and down the sides a bit. New skeletal material can only be produced by the coral's flesh, so only the parts of the skeleton that are covered can be added to, while the exposed areas are left "as is" for the duration of the coral's life.

Colonial stony corals may also have a partially covered skeleton where the colony is branched and the polyps live only at the end portions of each branch, but they may have completely enclosed skeletons as well. These are often relatively large aragonite structures with only a thin layer of tissue covering the entire surface, and the polyps are typically small compared to those of other types of stony corals. It may sound odd that smaller polyps form the larger skeletons, but when the entire skeleton is covered, the polyps can add more and more aragonite over the surface of the whole thing and increase the skeleton's size in all directions.

Many corals have skeletons that are only partially covered by tissue.

Part 1

As far as actual skeletal structure goes, regardless of whether a stony coral is colonial or not, or how much of the skeleton is covered, you'll notice the presence of numerous thin radiating structures called "septa." You can also look at the skeletons of colonial corals and often clearly see where one polyp stops and the next starts, with each polyp's area being called a "corallite." These can vary from being relatively widely spaced to very tightly spaced, and some can even be joined together in ways that prevent you from determining where the boundaries of each polyp/corallite are. This is because they might be so well-integrated that the polyps have no distinct beginning and end and may resemble one organism with many often oddly shaped mouths.

Branching corals are among the most sought after due to their attractive shape.

Coral Shapes

Each particular species of stony coral has one or more terms that can be used to describe its overall shape, how it grows, and how the polyps are arranged. Examples of these terms are: foliaceous (leaflike), columnar (rising columns) or dendroid (branching), but most can be described fairly easily in plain English without requiring you to learn so many new words. "Branched" means branched, and "dome-shaped" means the coral is shaped like a dome, etc. The only words that may be difficult to figure out are "massive" and "flabello-meandroid." "Massive" does not mean something is large, but instead simply means it grows as a mass with no particular form (although massive stony corals are most often boulder-like). "Flabello-meandroid," on the other hand, is a bit harder to put into words. In general, these types of corals are somewhat cone-shaped, flattened (flabellate), and curvy (meandroid) all at the same time.

Various species of "closed" brain corals grow in massive formations.

Coral Nutrition

Have you ever wondered why every time you see a picture of a coral reef it is located in clear, brightly lit water? It is because reef-building corals have millions of single-celled algae living within their tissues. These algae require bright light to perform photosynthesis; the bright light also allows the algae to have a very unusual relationship with

Zooxanthellae are green or brown, but corals can also produce many colorful pigments.

their coral hosts, called "symbiosis." In this type of relationship, both parties involved receive benefits from the other, and it is essential that you understand the basics of how it works.

The Role of Zooxanthellae

With the aid of the plentiful sunlight seen in clear, shallow reef environments, algae (properly called "zooxanthellae") carry out photosynthesis within the host's tissues and can produce excess quantities of nutritious simple sugars like glucose. These "leftovers" can then be donated to their host through a process aptly termed "translocation," and the zooxanthellae may produce so much excess sugar under optimal conditions that they can give over 90 percent of what they generate to the host and still have plenty for themselves. A host coral, in turn, may end up acquiring only a small percentage of its total nutrition through other means, such as prey capture (more on this in a moment). As a result, they rely much less on "real food" than other corals that don't have zooxanthellae.

Zooxanthellae can help corals grow much faster.

Nonsymbiotic corals (corals with no zooxanthellae) are well-known for their slow growth, as they build their skeletons at a snail's pace. However, zooxanthellae also play a significant role in the rate of production of aragonite skeletal material, allowing reef-building stony corals to grow at a more rapid pace. There are a couple of common explanations for this, the first having to do with the pH inside a coral's tissues.

Because the production of aragonite only works well at a relatively high pH, some believe that the zooxanthellae help keep the pH higher within a symbiotic coral. During photosynthesis, the zooxanthellae take in carbon dioxide (like all other photosynthetic organisms) from the host coral's tissues and produce oxygen in return, which is significant because an increase in the amount of carbon dioxide can make the pH go down in fluids. Thus, by helping to remove carbon dioxide from those tissues, the zooxanthellae could be making production easier.

Another possible reason could be the removal of excess phosphate. Phosphate is an important nutrient that a host takes in, but if concentrations get too high, the production of aragonite can be slowed considerably or even stopped. As a result, some have suggested that zooxanthellae help speed production by keeping phosphate levels at a minimum within the coral's tissues because they assimilate and use phosphate for themselves (like all other plants). Of course, the increased rate of aragonite production could be a combination of both processes, or it may be neither, as there may still be other undiscovered answers.

If the coral obtains sugars and consequently grows faster, what do zooxanthellae get out of the deal? It would seem that the hosting half of the symbiosis gets a lot more than the other half, but zooxanthellae do get a "home" inside the host. However, many types of single-celled algae live in the seas without hosts, so having a home probably isn't all there is to it.

Phosphate is essential for all plants, but it is in short supply in typical reef environments where the clear waters are relatively low in nutrients. In fact, the concentration of phosphate is so low around most reefs that most algae have a hard time trying to grow there. What little phosphate and other nutrients are present around reefs aren't just floating around in the water either; instead, they are trapped within the tissues of the various organisms on the reef. Therefore, when corals eat, even if they only eat a little, they bring these hard-to-get nutrients into their bodies, where some is taken up by the zooxanthellae. Conversely, the zooxanthellae would likely have a much more difficult time getting such nutrients from seawater themselves.

Living inside corals provides benefits for zooxanthellae, too.

Like other animals, corals also produce nitrogen-based compounds during metabolism that are given off as waste products. However, these can be yet another source of essential nutrients for plants. Zooxanthellae can use these compounds for themselves, after which they can also create different nitrogenous compounds that the host can use. In actuality, then, they recycle the stuff back and forth in different forms.

This cycling of phosphorous and nitrogen in usable forms is one of the basic ways that a coral can make things easier on the zooxanthellae, but there are other ways, too. For example, corals can produce specialized pigments that protect themselves and the zooxanthellae from overdoses of ultraviolet radiation. Such pigments can reflect or absorb damaging UV, which is a good thing since even corals and algae can get "sunburned" without such aids.

Let's get back to eating now. Corals can obtain a lot of their dietary requirements from zooxanthellae, but they can't get everything they need. Thus, they still need to acquire food and nutrients via other means. To do this, many corals have small tentacles around their mouths that are used to snare and eat plankton, tiny crustaceans, and similar food. Likewise, many other corals have numerous large and powerful tentacles used to capture

The tentacles of elegance corals are powerful food capturing devices.

relatively large prey, often including live fishes, in addition to the small stuff. That's not all, though, as many may use a thin layer of mucus over their bodies to catch tiny plankton and bacteria in a flypaper-like fashion, slowly slurping in and eating the mucus and all that it has collected. Lastly, many corals can simply absorb some required nutrients from the surrounding seawater directly into their tissues instead of getting those nutrients by eating food particles or prey, or getting them from zooxanthellae. As you can see, corals have many methods of tackling their requirements for food and nutrients, and many use more than one of these techniques.

Coral Weapons

Organisms require weapons of some kind or another for survival purposes, and while it may not always be obvious, corals are no exception by a long shot. Competition on reefs is vigorous to say the least, and corals must do everything they can to get food, protect themselves from predators, and make some living space for themselves.

Hiding among the polyps of this frogspawn coral are dangerous sweeper tentacles.

As I just mentioned, even though almost all of the corals found on reefs have zooxanthellae, they also depend to some degree or another upon the capture of prey and/or food particles ranging from microscopic bacteria and plankton to small fishes. In the close-packed reef environment, all must also attempt to fight off anything that might eat them and defend themselves against any competitors that might overgrow and kill them or grow up and over them, leaving them in the shade. If you rely on light-dependent zooxanthellae for a primary nutrient source, this is obviously a bad thing, even if your opponent never actually touches you. For this reason, many corals employ a range of weapons to ensure that they can hold their own and live to produce offspring.

Cnidocytes

The first and most common types of coral weapons are the cnidocytes, which are also frequently referred to as "nematocysts." Depending on the type of coral in question, they're typically located throughout the epidermis and are heavily concentrated in the stinging tentacles, which can give them a considerably extended range of use. In fact, they are oftentimes tightly compacted into packets or batteries along the tentacles in order to give a sting victim a relatively strong punch from just a light touch.

Each cnidocyte is covered with minute barbs and is basically just a single rounded cell that holds a tightly coiled tube inside that does the stinging. When held in the unfired position, the tube is tightly wound inside the cell and can be ejected outward like a tiny spring-loaded harpoon. The tube is closed at the far end in some cases and simply acts as an anchor or snare by means of the tiny barbs covering the surface. They may also be covered with a natural adhesive instead, allowing them to stick to whatever they touch, whether it be a prey item, a particle, or just a firm substrate to hold onto.

However, in other cases, the tube is hollow from end to end and a bit of toxin is pumped through it once the tube hits its victim. The toxin acts as a neurotoxin that causes paralysis in the victim, or it can damage the membranes of the cells it comes into contact with, killing them in the process. Either way, a small prey item will end up immobilized and then eaten.

The tubes are ejected when various stimuli affect a cnidocyte, the stimuli usually consisting of a combination of both physical touch and a chemical detection of flesh. The combination of the two to promote ejection helps to make sure that the cells aren't constantly being used up trying to sting an inanimate object like a rock or shell. This is important because each cnidocyte dies in the process of releasing its tube and isn't replaced for as long as a few days.

Sweeper Tentacles

Cnidocytes and tentacles are also used for other defensive purposes, as they can be unleashed in an effort to keep another coral from competing for available space. "Regular" tentacles can be used in this manner, but many corals also have specialized, even more elongated tentacles produced specifically for this job. These are

Digestive filaments can be used as weapons by some corals.

called "sweeper" tentacles, and they can easily be three or four times as long as the rest of the tentacles. Built to kill, they typically carry a higher number of cnidocytes as well.

As you read about specific types of corals, you may be surprised to learn that some of the least likely corals have these very deadly sweepers. Some corals will conspicuously have them all the time, but many others won't normally show any types of stinging tentacles at all and will extend them only after the lights go out. With this in mind, be careful where you place any type of coral that has stinging tentacles, and make sure to keep everyone else a minimum of at least several inches away.

Mesenterial Filaments

Another less obvious weapon is the use of structures called "mesenterial filaments," which are actually the numerous digestive structures found inside a coral's body. These light-colored, spaghetti-like ribbons of flesh are used to secrete digestive enzymes for breaking down food when it is taken in, but they can also be used for a couple of other jobs, too.

When a coral is growing and trying to take up more space, a

number of filaments can be ejected or spat out onto a surface to scour it free of algae or other organisms through the production of digestive enzymes. The caustic enzymes they produce quite literally melt away any exposed living tissues with which they might come into contact. As a defensive weapon, they can also be used by a coral that is irritated or under attack. Some corals can cover themselves with a tangled mess of mesenterial filaments, and when the stimuli that brought them out dissipate, the filaments are just pulled back into the body. Unlike stinging tentacles, these structures don't have much reach at all and shouldn't be too much of a concern when placing corals in your aquarium, as long as the different corals do not come into contact with each other.

Toxic Compounds

Some corals have developed yet another means of defending their territory and clearing new ground for growth: Many types of soft corals can exude a variety of toxic chemicals into the waters surrounding them. Many give off a weak but constant flow of nasty compounds that can irritate and stunt the growth of other types of corals growing nearby, some of which you may have heard of

Leather corals produce toxic substances that can adversly affect other corals in your Aquarium.

before. Compounds such as terpenoids, diterpenoids, and acetates can be used quite effectively, and any coral that is downcurrent from the emitter will be bathed in a lightly concentrated but never-ending flow of poison.

What makes this sort of thing such a headache is the fact that some corals react to these toxins very strongly, while many others don't seem to react to them at all. As a result, you may find that only one particular coral seems to be having difficulties in your aquarium and be led to believe that there is something "wrong" with that particular specimen, when really it is just more strongly affected by the chemicals its neighbors are giving off. The use of an effective skimmer and/or quality activated carbon will normally remove enough of these compounds from an aquarium's water to keep toxin concentrations from ever being a tankwide problem, but they might not always help the corals that may be in direct proximity to an emitter. Corals any closer than a few inches away may be killed (although this very rarely happens), while others that are within several inches may simply stay perpetually "unhappy." In fact, it is quite common to see various corals that normally expand a great deal, or that have small polyps that extend during the day, refuse to do so when placed downcurrent from some soft corals. Hence, many hobbyists will tell you that it is nearly impossible to keep various stony corals with large numbers of soft corals. Luckily, this is only the case when certain types of corals are mixed in aquariums with insufficient skimming or activated carbon filtration.

In still other situations when there is direct contact made between corals, this sort of chemical warfare can become much more aggressive. Various sorts of encrusting soft corals can "burn" many other corals they may come into contact with; again, this is without the use of stinging tentacles. Obviously, this can be a serious problem in the enclosed aquarium environment where such corals can grow quickly and overrun other inhabitants, killing almost anything in their paths. On many occasions, hobbyists have bragged about how well some of their rapidly growing, encrusting corals are doing in their tanks and how fast they are growing, only to discover later that the growth couldn't be stopped when it needed to be, leading to the death of another organism.

> ### Watch Out!
>
> As a last note, there are a few corals that may injure you to some degree. While some people react strongly and others may not react at all, you should be careful when contacting stony corals, just to be safe. For example, hammer, elegance, flowerpot, horn, and fire corals have all been known to irritate or even burn some unlucky hobbyists.

The lesson to learn from all of this is that you can't just stick corals in a tank next to each other any which way and expect to be successful. You'll have to read about each type you intend to buy, learn about its compatibilities with other corals, and act accordingly. Fortunately, with only minimal forethought, you can avoid almost all of these problems and save yourself and your corals a lot of trouble.

Coral Reproduction

Corals can reproduce in two fundamental ways: sexually and asexually. In case you've forgotten, this means that one method involves the production and mixing of sperm and eggs to form offspring and increase genetic diversity (sexual), while the other requires no such specialized cells (asexual). In addition, many species can

Zoanthids will reproduce and spread from one rock to another with little difficulty.

reproduce in a variety of specific ways, so to better understand them and figure out what you might expect to see, we'll take a quick look at both methods.

Sexual Reproduction

The basics are the same. Some sperm produced by a male meet up with some eggs produced by a female, and fertilization occurs. For corals, though, the process doesn't end here. The whole story is actually quite interesting because corals can be a single sex, both sexes at the same time, or sometimes one sex now and the other later. Different types may carry out fertilization internally or externally, as well.

About one fourth of all corals are gonochoric, meaning they produce just sperm or just eggs, and are thus considered to be just male or just female. However, the rest of the corals are hermaphroditic, meaning they can produce sperm and eggs and are both male and female. This may or may not occur simultaneously. If some of the polyps in a colony are male while other polyps are female at the same time, they are called "simultaneous hermaphrodites." But, in some cases, all of the polyps may be male at one point and then later change to female; this is called "protandry." (They're protandric hermaphodites.) Or, the opposite can occur and they can all be female and then male, which is called "protogyny." (They're protogynic hermaphrodites.) Switching sexes may sound far out, but keep in mind that there are a few other organisms that do so–a coral's reproductive system is actually exceptionally simple.

In addition to these differences in sexual orientation, about one sixth of corals are brooders, meaning they carry out fertilization internally. The rest are broadcast spawners that spew sperm and eggs into the environment, sometimes by the millions. When fertilization occurs inside a brooder, the product is larvae that grow for a while before being released. However, when fertilization in the case of spawners occurs, the larvae are on their own from the beginning.

If larvae are brooded and allowed to grow a bit, then they are already able to settle to the bottom, attach, and begin to form a new coral when released. They also already have a bit of zooxanthellae from the parent and can start reaping the benefits of photosynthesis at once. Conversely, larvae that result from spawning must go through a metamorphosis in the environment before they are able to settle and grow, and they also must contract their own sample of zooxanthellae. This might sound like a big disadvantage, but it allows them to do something that brooded larvae don't. They can drift for weeks or even months and can settle in areas far from their parents, allowing them to greatly increase their geographical distribution.

Asexual Reproduction

If you thought sexual reproduction was complicated, look at what's coming! Through asexual reproduction, corals may reproduce themselves in even more ways without the need for sperm and eggs. These are simple methods that require little or no use of energy, but the downside is that all offspring produced asexually are nothing more than genetically identical clones of their parents. This

Pieces of mushroom anemones often tear away from large specimens, only to grow into a new mushroom.

is not a good way to increase diversity, but it does increase numbers nonetheless.

Asexual reproduction begins with plain old fission. This occurs when a species of soft coral literally splits itself down the middle and makes two half-sized versions of the original. It's similar to cellular reproduction (but on a very different scale, of course), where both products have all the parts they need in order to feed, grow, and reproduce effectively. Next comes pedal laceration, which is a type of auto-fragmentation (breaking one's self up) that is similar to fission. The difference is that while fission tends to produce two individuals that are roughly the same size, only a small part of the parent is pinched off during laceration. The term "pedal" refers to a foot, which is quite appropriate because the part that is pinched away is actually a section of a soft coral's base of attachment. This is typically done as the parent slowly creeps away and lets a small section of itself stay behind, attached to a rock or other surface. Eventually, the piece tears away and then develops into a new coral. As another means of auto-fragmentation, various soft corals can also pinch off sections of their branches at times. The bits then drop to the bottom, attach, and form new corals in a process aptly called "branch dropping."

Stony corals have skeletons that prevent them from doing this, but external forces can fragment these and soft corals as well. In such cases, forces such as predators, storms, anchors, and aquarium hobbyists can break or cut away sections of corals, which can then grow into new ones. The pieces, often called "frags," just settle, stick, and grow.

Stony corals can also produce small versions of themselves called "polyp buds" or "balls." These are small amounts of tissue that grow from a parent until they are large enough or heavy enough to break away. They often form at the edge of a coral's body where the skeleton is exposed, and they often have a small skeleton forming inside at the time of separation as well. In a similar fashion, a few corals can produce very small but complete versions of themselves (with a skeleton included) called "anthocauli" on their upper surfaces. Anthocauli are often formed after an injury occurs or disease strikes as a last ditch effort to produce a few offspring in case death is imminent.

At times, a single polyp or a few polyps of a stony coral may simply separate themselves from the skeleton and drift away. These polyps are then carried

Many corals can start off as single polyps but will soon grow into large colonies.

away by currents and settle to form a whole new skeleton elsewhere in the ocean. This process is called "polyp bailout," and it's also often a response to disturbances such as a boat slamming into a coral reef, a diver breaking off a piece of a stony coral, or even a large fish slamming into the corals.

Reproduction in Aquariums

Aquariums obviously aren't the sea, so you can't expect things to go exactly the same way inside them. Corals very rarely spawn in aquariums, and we can't figure out exactly why that is. While the timing of spawning events on reefs often seems to be tied to lunar cycles, changes in the number of daylight hours, or a few other things, turning on a light of some sort at night to simulate a full moon and other attempts to induce spawning have proved useless. Nevertheless, it does occur at times. Will you end up with a tank full of a gazillion baby corals? More than likely, the answer is no, as nearly 100 percent of any coral larvae produced are either eaten, killed by a pump, or removed by some sort of filtering device. As a result, it is uncommon to find new corals growing after spawning takes place.

Coral reproduction in aquariums is typically only asexual.

However, many thriving stony corals will frequently produce polyp buds/balls in aquariums, so keep an eye on their undersides. They may also produce anthocauli and/or go through polyp bailout if stressed or injured, and on some occasions may do either for no apparent reason. Unless you have some storm-like waves or coral-munching fishes in your aquarium, you won't be seeing any fragmentation other than auto-fragmentation, which is actually fairly common. For this reason, keep an eye out for dropped-off pieces, too.

Part Two
The Basics of Coral Husbandry

"Having a bad hair day, Ted?"

Water Quality

There are quite a few things to think about and take care of before you'll be ready to bring any corals home. You need to know what's required for all corals in general, make a plan for your own aquarium, and then get everything up and running before you even think about bringing corals home. With this in mind, I'll run

Flowerpot corals will need premium water quality to have a chance at survival in captivity.

through the basics of what corals need with respect to their aquarium environment and what you'll need to do for them. The details of aquarium set-up and long-term aquarium maintenance are beyond the scope of this book, but this should be enough to point you in the right direction and get you started.

First of all, as is the case with any aquarium, you need to maintain good water quality. This essentially means that, in order to keep your sea creatures alive, you need to have the water in the aquarium close in character to natural seawater. Contrary to what many naïve beginners may believe, mixing up some synthetic sea salt mix and water and then pouring it in the tank is just the beginning when it comes to reef aquariums. Let's take a look at the important parameters of water quality that you'll need to pay close attention to.

Salinity/Specific Gravity

The water must be kept within an acceptable range of salinity, which means you must make sure that there is an appropriate amount of synthetic salt mix dissolved in it. You'll need to use a hydrometer of some sort to test your specific gravity and keep it in the ideal range of 1.023 to 1.027. Too far above or below this range will quickly result in total failure, even if all other parameters are perfect.

Temperature

You'll need to make sure the water stays somewhere in the neighborhood of 70°F to 82°F and doesn't shift rapidly one way or another. Temperatures may get higher or lower than this in natural environments, but many corals will drop dead at just a few degrees over or under this range; thus, it's a bad idea to push them any closer to their limits. A temperature range of 75°F to 80°F is really the optimal range you should shoot for, as this is perfectly suitable and gives some room for the unforeseen (and hopefully short-lived) air conditioning or heater outage. Temperatures around reefs also change very slowly, over periods of weeks or months, not so much from day to night. This is why stability is important.

You will also need to have plenty of live rock and/or live sand to ensure that your aquarium has adequate biological filtration to remove toxic ammonia and nitrate produced by fishes, other organisms, and the breakdown of dead matter. Concentrations of both of these substances must be maintained at zero.

Chemical Composition

Calcium concentrations, pH, and alkalinity must be maintained at acceptable levels as well. Many corals use calcium from seawater to produce their aragonite skeletons or skeletal components. This means you'll need to make sure they have access to plenty of calcium. Coral health and skeletal growth are strongly influenced by the pH of the aquarium's water, too, which is strongly affected by the water's alkalinity. Specifically, alkalinity refers to the ability of your aquarium to resist any changes in pH, which are unwanted. Remember, stability is golden.

For these reasons, calcium concentrations will need to be maintained in the range of 400 to 450 ppm. The pH should be kept optimally in the range of 8.2 to 8.4 (although it often gets a little higher or lower). Lastly, the alkalinity will need to be kept in the range of 7 to 12 dKH. Fortunately, there are many ways to accomplish all of this, from kalkwasser additions, to 2-part additives, to the use of a device called a "calcium reactor," all of which have their own pros and cons. You'll have to decide which best suits your wallet and your habits.

Aside from all of this, you'll also need to keep nutrient levels low, especially phosphate. Most corals come from areas where available nutrients come in the form of food but are not found dissolved in the water itself. Thus, the concentration of dissolved phosphate on reefs is very low, and you should strive to keep it that way in your aquarium. As mentioned earlier, the concentration of phosphate has a strong effect on the production of aragonite and too much can make things difficult. It also acts as a good fertilizer for unwanted algal growth that can really muck up your tank. As a result, you'll need to refrain from overfeeding your fishes and corals (the primary source for phosphate); you will also need to employ the use of water changes and/or a skimmer and/or algal filtration. Again, all of these methods of nutrient control have their own pros and cons, and you'll have to decide which is best for you.

Circulation & Current

Because corals lack any type of gills or blood, they rely on the absorption of oxygen to stay alive. Thus, they need a constant bath of oxygenated seawater. They also rely on currents to bring them food, to keep sediment from settling on and smothering them, and to blow away wastes. As you can see, water movement is very important to their survival.

Powerheads provide good circulation in reef aquariums.

Some corals need more circulation than others, but in general, they all require much more water motion than what is seen in many "regular" aquariums, such as those that have nothing more than an undergravel filter or maybe a box-type power-filter hanging off the back. You'll need to use pumps of some sort or another to keep the water moving around–the more turbulent it is, the better. In general, more than one pump should be used, and they should be positioned in such a way that their effluent streams intersect and create mixing currents that move around the tank. You can also buy electronic devices that act like timers; these switch different pumps on and off in sequences to create mixing currents.

Part 2

7

Lighting

Because symbiotic corals require lighting of sufficient quality and intensity for their zooxanthellae to produce food, you'll need a powerful lighting system with bulbs designed for this purpose. The three basic types of these systems utilize V.H.O. (very high output) fluorescent bulbs, P.C. (power-compact) fluorescent bulbs, or M.H. (metal

Zoanthids need good lighting in order to thrive and reproduce in reef aquariums.

Metal halide lighting is one of the best ways to provide corals with their required lighting needs.

halide) bulbs, and many of them also use a combination of these. Various systems also have differing numbers of them as well.

Intensity

Different symbiotic corals will need varying amounts of light in order to thrive. Some need low intensity, some need moderate intensity, and others need high intensity illumination. However, while the intensity obviously depends on the specific type of coral in question, the generally accepted lowest intensity lighting system that can be used for keeping any of them alive would be something like a couple of V.H.O. or P.C. lights over a medium-sized tank, like a standard 55 gallon. Of course, the same sort of set-up would be considered "moderate intensity" over a much shallower tank, like a 20 or 30 gallon, and considered unacceptable over a much deeper tank, like a 150 gallon, as light quickly diminishes with increasing water depth. Likewise, four V.H.O. or power compact bulbs over a 55-gallon tank could be considered "moderate intensity" or "high intensity" over a smaller tank, or "low intensity" over a larger/deeper tank. For the most part, I'd say nothing less than a set-up that includes M.H. bulbs can be considered "high intensity" for medium and large tanks, and some folks even use them over tanks as small as 20 gallons (which might be considered "super-duper intensity").

Watts per Gallon Ratio

It's easy to see that intensity varies greatly with depth, but keep in mind that it can also vary greatly from the center to the sides, so the deeper and/or wider the tank is, the more the lighting intensity can vary from location to location inside it. Many people use a general "watt per gallon" ratio when trying to characterize their set-up, with 4 watts/gallon being the minimum acceptable ratio. However, this variance in intensity from top to bottom and center to side means the watt/gallon ratio doesn't always work so well.

For example, if I say I have four 110-watt V.H.O. bulbs over a 55-gallon tank, that would be 440 total watts for 55 gallons or 8 watts/gallon–double the minimum ratio and quite satisfactory for almost anything you'd ever want to keep. You can be sure that with such a ratio in a tank of moderate depth, even the corals at the very bottom will get plenty of light. On the other hand, what if I had a 240-gallon tank that was more than twice as wide and almost twice as deep? Even if I had four 250-watt metal halides and four

Many hobbyists like the look of coralline algae. These algae seem to do best with heavy actinic blue lighting.

165-watt V.H.O. tubes for 6.9 watts/gallon, corals at the bottom front edge of the tank would be getting far less light than anything in that 55-gallon tank, even though the watt/gallon number is close to the same. From the other point of view, what about 4 watts/gallon over a tank that's only 6 inches deep? The ratio is much lower, but everything would be situated within just a few inches of the bulbs themselves. Thus, they would be rather well illuminated.

Now that I've just showed you that the "watts per gallon" rule doesn't really work, I have to tell you that it's still the best way available to common hobbyists in judging if you are providing appropriate illumination for your corals. As advancements are made, this rule of thumb will surely be improved upon. You just have to use your best judgment and think about how lighting changes in different areas in your tank and what can go where. I call it a light equivalence, and I also consider what the approximate watt/gallon ratio would be for a given location in a tank, rather than for the whole tank. In other words, if a tank is 30 inches deep and has 9 watts/gallon, that ratio would be considered high intensity (9 or more watts/gallon) only in the upper portion.

Foods & Feeding

Various types of corals may occasionally capture some fish food moving around in an aquarium, but there are also three basic ways to provide foods specifically for them. You can hand-feed them, you can add some sort of store-bought "plankton in a bottle" or a plankton substitute product, or you can set up your aquarium

Many corals often need feedings of invertebrate foods to supplement their photosynthetic capabilities.

in such a way as to provide them with natural foods generated in a deep bed of sand within the tank itself.

Feeding By Hand

Corals that have large enough polyps/mouths, especially those with relatively large feeding tentacles, can be fed by hand. Almost without exception, they'll take small meaty foods such as brine shrimp, bloodworms, or bits of clams and squid, etc. Larger corals will take small fishes, too. Thus, all you need to do for the small stuff is find a large syringe at the local drugstore and remove the needle, or you can go to a veterinarian and get an even larger one. Armed with the syringe, just thaw out some frozen brine shrimp, etc. in a small glass with some water from the tank, stir up the mix, and then suck up a dose. (If the hole in the end of your syringe is too small, just use some scissors and cut off part of the tip.) Before you get started though, I'll mention that I find it very helpful to briefly turn off all of the pumps, powerheads, and anything else that creates currents in the aquarium so the foods aren't blown away. You just can never forget to turn them back on! You should also give your fishes a good feeding first so that they don't steal all of the food from the intended recipients. You'll quickly discover that any coral with

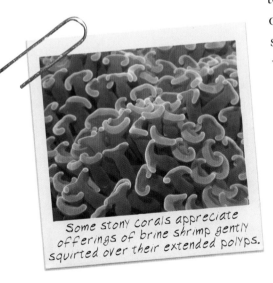

Some stony corals appreciate offerings of brine shrimp gently squirted over their extended polyps.

relatively large tentacles will quickly snatch up anything you squirt into them with your syringe, and numerous sorts of gorgonians, button polyps, mushroom anemones, and other critters will do the same. However, there are a few corals won't, and figuring out which ones will and which won't is often a matter of trial and error.

If you watch closely enough, you should also notice that some of the corals that don't normally have noticeable tentacles or mouths will often "open up" when foods are added to the water. They detect the presence of the food and can slowly extend their feeding tentacles that are often retracted and out of sight during the day. Once you figure this out, you can take better care of them: squirt a bit of food over them, wait a minute for them to extend their hidden tentacles, and then give them a bigger dose of food. Actually, just a little liquid from a syringe will get them excited.

Feeding With Plankton

Almost all corals capture plankton of various sorts and sizes, and there are a number of products you can use to provide corals with the real thing or at least a suitable substitute to help them out. There are liquid additives, which consist of real plankton in water, that are very popular, but there are also a few powdered products that can work well, too. For the powdered stuff, just scoop out some tank water and mix it with some of the powder, and then pour it back into the aquarium. Aside from telling you to follow the manufacturer's directions for whatever you may choose to use, I'll also point out that these additives are typically useful for all sorts of corals. Even those corals that have large polyps and/or big tentacles will still capture small foods, as will many of those that have minute tentacles, or even none.

If you want to provide your corals with a steady supply of live foods from within the aquarium, you can set it up with a deep sand bed that is full of organisms (which is known as the D.S.B. method of aquarium-keeping). You'll need to do a little extra homework to set one up and maintain it properly, but in a nutshell, all you'll be doing is using 3 or 4 inches of fine aragonite sand to fill the bottom of the tank, and then stocking it with sand-dwelling critters. The organisms that live in the sand bed can become a food source for your corals, but more importantly, they are constantly producing eggs, larvae, etc. that are released into the water. Here, many are captured and eaten, thus providing an excellent supplement to any regular feedings that you are offering.

Part Three
Propagating Corals in Your Aquarium

"Jim don't take this the wrong way, but have you ever considered growing something other than Elkhorn Coral?"

Propagation

As covered earlier, many of the corals you can keep in your aquarium have the ability to reproduce asexually by means of fission and/or fragmentation. This ability can also be used to spread them around an aquarium, too. This practice is called "propagation" and is essentially nothing more than intentionally breaking or

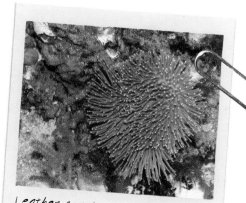

Leather corals are fairly easy to propagate in home aquariums.

cutting up corals as a means of making more of them.

Before starting, keep in mind that your aquarium must have excellent water quality, and you must have very healthy specimens to work with. If you don't, you'll likely end up with nothing but a bunch of cut and broken dead corals. There are numerous little tricks of the trade that you can learn by doing some homework down the road, but I'll run through the basics to get you off to a good start. I also recommend that you wear some eye protection when performing any of the following techniques, as the chemicals that many soft and leather corals produce may end up just about anywhere when specimens are being cut. For the same reasons, this sort of work should be done outside the aquarium when possible.

Mushrooms are probably the easiest of all the "soft corals" to use for propagation projects.

Mushrooms

As far as techniques and tools go, mushroom anemones can be the easiest of all to propagate, so they are a good place to start. All you need to do is slice them down the middle with a razor blade. It's a one-tool job (the razor) that can be performed quickly and easily right in the aquarium, as you are unlikely to experience any adverse effects by carrying out the procedure elsewhere. While cutting living things in half may initially sound like a recipe for disaster, I assure you that if they are healthy to begin with, very few halves, if any, will die from this procedure.

Now, if you want to place them somewhere else, instead of cutting the mushrooms in such a way as to make two equal halves, you will need to cut them through the base and remove their "caps". This won't kill them either, and the bases will slowly grow new caps and return to normal. In the meantime, you can use the severed caps (which are typically referred to as "cuttings" at this point) to start new mushrooms elsewhere. All you'll need are some pieces of seashell, rock, or other suitable substrate to work with, a couple of containers of aquarium water (which you should pour down the drain when finished), a few paper towels, and a tube of gel-type "superglue" (cyanoacrylate glue).

To make things as easy as possible, keep all the caps on hold in one container of aquarium water. Squeeze out a relatively small glob of glue onto a piece of dry substrate, and stick a cap onto the glob right side up, after carefully dabbing the bottom of the cap on a paper towel. Let the cap set for just a second and then carefully place the piece into the second container of aquarium water. The glue gets hot as it hardens, so the real trick is to wait long enough to get the glue to grab hold of the mushroom cap without letting it get so hot that it damages it. Once it is submerged in the second container, this won't be a problem, and I'd say the most difficult part of this procedure is gluing the cap to the substrate instead of to your fingers.

Part 3

The glue will continue to harden underwater and usually does a good job of holding the caps in place. As a result, you can usually remove the newly made pieces from the container and place them right back into the aquarium after the glue has completely set. The water won't affect the glue, but mushrooms are known to produce copious amounts of mucous slime (especially when injured), so at times you may have trouble getting the glue to hold. In such cases, you can cover the specimen with a piece of tulle mesh/netting. This can be found at material shops and is essentially nothing but an inexpensive, net-like material that won't degrade in saltwater.

The mesh can be pre-cut with scissors, draped over a cap and the substrate, and then secured with a little more glue or a rubber band. Then the whole piece can be placed in the aquarium, with the mesh kept in place until the cap has a firm hold on the substrate. It can then be removed and reused or discarded. You just need to be careful that you don't squeeze the cap too tightly under the mesh or have it so loose that the cap doesn't stay in contact with the substrate. You also need to make sure that the new piece gets sufficient water movement around it and through the mesh to keep the cap cleaned of slime and/or debris.

Colonial Polyps

Encrustors like button polyps, sea mats, star polyps, *Xenia*, etc. aren't much more difficult to work with than mushrooms, but they are different in that they live as colonies and so are typically joined together by a common fleshy base. This is not a problem, though, as these encrustors can be easily propagated using two basic procedures. The first is to cut and break up colonies and glue the pieces elsewhere (using some mesh if needed), while the second is to let them encrust an object and then just cut away and move the object elsewhere. The stalked varieties of *Xenia* can be cut apart at their bases like other species, but they can also be "decapitated" like mushrooms.

Leather Corals

Finger and tree leather corals are easy, too, as cuttings as small as half-inch bits can be clipped from the tips of any branch. Conversely, you can cut a piece as large as the entire top of a colony, leaving the trunk to grow new branches. In any case, the technique is still essentially the same. You can glue the cuttings to pieces of substrate, and use mesh if needed.

Toadstool leather corals tend to have a large trunk, which is topped with a cap instead of branches, but you can lop off the entire cap and the trunk will grow a new one. You can also make smaller cuttings by snipping away pieces of the cap. Any size cutting can be used and will relatively quickly develop into a new individual, complete with a

Cuttings made from leather corals can easily be attached to rocks using glue.

trunk and cap of its own. The only special advice I would give is that when working with any of these, you should try to make clean cuts and glue the cut surface to the substrate, leaving the undamaged surface exposed.

Gorgonians

Gorgonians are just as easy, with just about any size piece being useable. Cuttings can be glued to a substrate, and I've even been able to stick cuttings in small holes in live rock without using any glue. The only thing in particular to note is that they have a very tough, plastic-like rod that runs through the center of each branch, so you'll need some very sharp scissors to make a clean cut.

Stony Corals

When it comes to stony corals, larger-polyped branched species that have polyps and flesh only at the ends of their branches are easy to propagate. All you'll need to do is carefully remove a branch and glue it elsewhere. Depending on the size of the branches, you can use a pair of heavy scissors to crunch through, or even better, you can use a fine saw. You can use the superglue for gluing, but for larger specimens you may want to use aquarium-safe underwater epoxy cement. A number of these are available, and they work great.

Small-polyped stony corals aren't much more difficult. These types of corals can be broken up manually or by using some heavy snips and each piece (now called a "frag") can be used to start a new colony. You'll want to do your best to make clean breaks, but the

size of the "frag" is almost irrele-
vant. Again, you can use pieces as
small as half an inch if you like, or
you can break off whole branches
or clusters of branches.

Once you make the cuttings, the
rest of the procedure is the same.
Quickly dab the exposed part of
the skeleton where the break is,
and then glue the cutting onto a
piece of suitable substrate. Also
note that while it is much easier
to do this sort of work outside of
the aquarium, it isn't necessary
when working with stony
corals. While these corals may
give off copious quantities of mucus when irritated, they
don't emit doses of toxins into the water. Thus, it is possible to
simply reach in, snap off a branch, and then take it out to work with.

Unhealthy Stony Corals can often be salvaged by manually breaking off the living parts into "frags."

Now that you see how easy propagation can really be, I want to
stress the fact that all successful hobbyists should try it for a number of reasons. Obviously, you can make your aquarium look better
and fuller without spending as much money on specimens while
simultaneously reducing our impact on the world's reefs, but these
aren't the only benefits. In addition, propagated coral specimens

Young "frags" often grow at an amazingly high rate if they are given what they need.

(fishes, too) have demonstrated time and time again that they tend to be much hardier than wild caught/collected ones. Many corals that are well-known for their fickleness in aquariums, and especially those that ship poorly, are often tough as nails if raised in an aquarium from a cutting/frag. It seems that they adapt better growing in captivity if they start small. Lastly, propagation can also be very enjoyable and interesting activity, much like raising a garden. You get to sow the seeds and watch what happens. While things may not go exactly as planned at times, success is very rewarding and can pay off emotionally and monetarily.

Part Four
Guide to Common Corals

"I think my Tooth Coral has a cavity."

Gaining an Understanding

Now we're ready to take a closer look at the common types of corals and how to best care for each of them. There are far more species available than what I've covered in the following two chapters, but the information pertains to most of those corals you'll regularly see at local shops. The various types covered in Chapters 11

Various species of brain corals are commonly encountered in aquarium shops.

and 12 are listed by their most popular common names, and for each type of coral you'll find the information set forth below.

Common Names

A coral's common name is exactly that–the nonscientific or popular name by which the coral is known. For some reason, this often has no apparent relation to what a coral looks like and often varies depending on whether you are asking a fisherman, a diver, or an aquarist what something is called. For this reason, don't fret if you call a type of coral one name and see it called something different somewhere else. Many corals have more than one common name amongst the members of the aquarium hobby. This is why it's always a good idea to know the scientific name of a coral if you are trying to find more information about it, attempting to tell someone else what it is, or endeavoring to order one from a list without a picture.

Scientific Names

For each common type of coral covered, there is at least one genus name given, which you'll see in italics. Also, there can be more than one genus name given in cases when similar corals that are actually in separate genera go by the same common name. Likewise, there are instances when several species are all called the same common name, or conversely, when scientists haven't decided on a species name yet. You can figure it out as you look at each type, but just remember that "sp." means the species is unknown or undetermined, while "spp." means there are several species represented in the same genera.

Descriptions

The descriptions I've provided are quite general, but to go into detail about every possible shape and color of each type of coral could take a whole (very large) book in itself. Almost any given coral is highly variable in form and color, but for the most part there are some basic characteristics and colors they commonly exhibit, which I've listed. If you should happen to find a green specimen when I didn't list green as an option for that type, it's likely just an unusual color form and probably not some unknown new species that you can name after yourself. Of course, if it's too brightly colored, it may in fact be dyed that way to make it more attractive or to mask health problems (more on that later in the section that covers shopping for specimens).

For those types of corals that are represented by more than one genus or species, I've also tried to give some tips on how to distinguish one species from another when it can be done easily, with some degree of reliability. Of course, there are many times when it takes a microscopic examination of the skeleton or some other such test to tell two different species apart, so at other times I've made no distinction between them.

Lighting

Ah, lighting again. For reef aquariums, this is obviously one of the most important things to think about and one of the most difficult things to deal with at the same time. As covered earlier, you'll need some bright lights, but how bright they need to be for various corals is highly variable. As you'll see, there are a few corals that can do just fine in relatively low light, some that can take just about any light, and others that require nothing less than full-intensity lighting.

As mentioned, there is no proven, definite way to determine exactly what low, moderate, and high intensity really mean, but you need to have at least a basic idea of what a particular coral can tolerate. For each type, I've provided a general range of intensity they can handle and some extra notes or information where applicable. Again, for corals that can live with low intensity lighting, you should provide no less than an equivalence of 4 or 5 watts/gallon. For moderate intensity, I'd try for something like an equivalence of 6 to 8 watts/gallon. For high intensity, you should provide an equivalence of around 9 or 10 watts/gallon or more. If anything, in each situation I suggest you err somewhat on the bright side if you have to, as corals can typically adapt to more intense lighting more readily than to less intense lighting.

Current

Corals come from many depths and also come from areas with greatly varying currents. Corals in shallow lagoons may never experience a current any stronger than the slow movement of the tides coming in and out, while those on a reef crest may be blasted by full-strength sea waves day and night. Thus, you'll need to make sure that each specimen gets enough current, but not too much. Many cannot stay free of sediment or feed if the current is too low, while others will not expand their soft tissues or feed if it is too strong.

For corals that prefer low currents, all you need to do is make sure that water is constantly flowing over them, albeit gently–just enough water to keep them free of sediment will do. Corals that thrive in moderate currents should be provided with a stronger flow but still shouldn't be placed directly in front of a powerhead or pump return. Conversely, corals that thrive in higher, stronger current areas can be placed in direct currents from pumps.

While the actual strength of current that various corals will enjoy is highly variable, a surging/turbulent type of flow is always best. Whether a coral prefers low, moderate, or high flow, you should try to avoid a set-up that directs water at the same rate and in the same direction at all times. For best results, try for a set-up that makes the water swirl and stir turbulently around the corals.

Feeding

Almost all corals will benefit from some sort of feeding or another, but each type can have preferences when it comes to what they'll take. Some like fine particulate foods, while others will enjoy larger, meaty foods and/or live fishes. Thus, I've given a bit of information about what you should provide for each type of coral.

Compatibility

In this section, I've gone over which species of corals can be in close proximity to others and which ones need to be separated from the rest of the reef. Often, these aggressive species can be separated using rocks or other hard materials so there stinging cells

Part 4

cannot damage the other residents. Remember that many corals have longer and deadlier tentacles than you might realize, while others have even more powerful sweeper tentacles made specifically for the purpose of killing any nearby competition. Still other corals give off a constant stream of noxious chemicals that can annoy, weaken, or even kill other corals in an aquarium.

Placement

Even if you find a spot where the lighting and current are right and the neighborhood is okay, this still may not be the best location for a specimen. Many corals have particular needs when it comes to where they should sit in an aquarium, so I've given a few tips when applicable. In cases when one should be placed on the bottom, on a soft/fine-grained substrate, you'll have the best luck doing exactly that. You should provide this type of coral with a layer of fine aragonite sand to sit upon, and you should not place it on a piece of live rock or on coarse, angular gravel. You may be able to place such a specimen on bare glass or on a rock and get away with it, but doing your best to re-create its natural environment is a good way to increase your chances of success. Likewise, those corals that are always found attached to hard substrates should be placed accordingly and set into a stable area of rockwork, or better yet, glued in a suitable location.

Reproduction/Propagation

Some corals may reproduce in an aquarium, but most will not. Some corals can be propagated, some cannot. Here I've given a little information on if and how various corals can reproduce on their own and whether or not and how you can reproduce them yourself if you choose to.

Hardiness

Many corals have poor survival rates during collection and shipping. Others may ship perfectly well but often cannot be maintained in tanks for more than a few months no matter what you try. Some are overly prone to suffer from disease even after being established, while others seem to be extremely sturdy. I've provided a few notes on what you might expect for each type of coral as far as survivability goes. Unfortunately, every specimen enjoys at least a slightly different life in nature and has a different experience when being collected, shipped, and sold. Likewise, the environment inside every aquarium is at least slightly different. There are always exceptions, and you may find that a coral that is supposed to be hardy drops dead, while one that you were wary of buying ends up flourishing. My advice is not to push your luck, and as a beginner, don't get it in your head that you can keep everything alive through extra attention, maintenance, etc. If I tell you a coral is unlikely to survive, it's because it is unlikely to survive and has proven so through the years in the aquariums of many caring hobbyists and experts alike.

Other Information

In this portion, I will talk about anything else I can think of that strikes me as important or maybe just plain interesting.

Part 4

Soft Corals

The term "soft coral' essentially refers to any group of corals that don't precipitate an external calcium-based skeleton. This description is rather informal and many serious reefers don't use it any longer but we will use it here because it is a good term for beginners to become familiar with. When describing soft corals, try to remember their common group names.

Soft corals alone can make a very impressive reef display.

Common Mushroom Anemones

Discosoma spp.

Description: Common mushrooms are solitary polyps that often look much like real mushrooms, with short stalks and flattened tops called a "disc," which can grow to sizes of up to 3 inches or so in diameter. Most are smooth, but others may have bumps or pimples covering their upper surfaces, and you can find them in about every color, many often having some fluorescence as well. Many also have polka dots or stripes and can be exceptionally beautiful. They are often found attached to hard substrates in large aggregations that are sometimes composed of mixes of different varieties.

Lighting: They can tolerate a broad range of lighting intensities and are well-known for their ability to thrive in areas that would seem to be too dark for almost any symbiotic coral.

Current: They prefer low current and will be folded over and unhappy in anything much stronger.

Feeding: Common mushrooms have a tiny bump of a mouth, no feeding tentacles, and won't take any foods given by hand. However, they will benefit from additions of plankton-type foods and/or a D.S.B. setup, as they feed by trapping tiny food particles in mucous coatings they produce over their discs.

Compatibility: Most are harmless and can grow right up against other corals. However, many others are able to irritate things they come into contact with. Always use caution when attempting to mix them.

Placement: They can go practically anywhere the current isn't too strong, but I suggest you try to keep them from coming into direct contact with other corals.

Reproduction/Propagation: They can be cut in a number of ways as a means of propagation. They also regularly reproduce on their own through fission and pedal laceration, forming large colonies.

Hardiness: They are typically some of the hardiest corals you can put in an aquarium. However, for unknown reasons, they will remain shriveled and sickly at times.

Other Info: They aren't really anemones! It's just a common name that has stuck, but is nonetheless incorrect. Also, the names *Discosoma* and *Actinodiscus* are treated as interchangeable and/or separate at times, and sometimes *Discosoma* is even used as a replacement for *Actinodiscus*. The name seems to depend on which taxonomist you ask.

Hairy Mushrooms (also called Tonga, Bull's-eye, or Metallic Mushrooms)

Rhodactis spp.

Description: There are several types of hairy mushrooms that are highly variable in size and appearance. However, there is one unifying characteristic they share, which is a disc that is completely covered on its upper surface by unusual tentacles. Other than that, some may reach a full size of only a couple of inches across, while others can easily reach a foot. And, like the "regular" mushrooms, they can come in more colors and patterns than I care to list.

There are a couple of particularly common varieties, the first of which is the "regular" hairy mushroom. These can get quite large (over 1 foot in diameter at times), and elaborate, finely branching tentacles often cover them. They come in several colorations, which include brown, cream, blue, and pink, and many also have bright fluorescent green mixed in, in which case they are often called "metallics" (instead of "fluorescents"). The others often go by the names Tonga and/or Bull's-eye mushrooms and only get up to 2 or maybe 3 inches at best. They usually come in blue, purple, or green, and they don't have much for tentacles. Those tentacles they do have are very interesting and surprisingly complex when observed up close. They look like tiny warty cauliflower heads or knobs and are quite unique.

Lighting: They can be kept under a broad range of lighting, from low to high intensity, but will prefer low to moderate intensity.

Current: They prefer low current and will be folded over and unhappy in anything much stronger.

Feeding: You may have to experiment a little, but most will take small meaty foods if hand-fed. This is especially true of those that have larger, more complex tentacles, while those that have little more than rough bumps for tentacles may take nothing. Those that eat will close up around food items as if there were a drawstring around their margin, slowly engulfing whatever they can fit in their mouths. Regardless, all will likely benefit from additions of plankton-type foods and/or a D.S.B. setup.

Compatibility: Many can burn other corals they come into contact with through the production of toxic compounds. Those that have larger tentacles may also use them to sting corals. Conversely, depending on what they come up against, the stings of other corals may injure them.

Placement: They can be situated practically anywhere the current isn't too strong but should be prevented from coming into direct contact with other corals. Also, keep in mind how big some of them can get as they grow.

Reproduction/Propagation: They can be cut in a number of ways as a means of propagation. They also regularly reproduce on their own through fission and pedal laceration and can even sometimes form large colonies.

Hardiness: They are typically some of the hardiest corals you can put in an aquarium, often being even more successful than other mushrooms.

Elephant Ear Mushrooms

Amplexidiscus fenestrafer

Description: These are exceptionally large mushrooms that easily reach diameters in the neighborhood of 1 foot. They are typically brown to greenish in color, have a large but short base attached to a hard substrate, and have numerous short tentacles on their upper surface. They also have a relatively large, centrally located mouth and are often found in small groups.

Lighting: They can thrive under a broad range of lighting, from low to high intensity.

Current: They prefer low current and will be folded over and unhappy in anything much stronger.

Feeding: They will require being fed meaty foods regularly (every few days optimally) and may benefit from additions of plankton-type foods and/or a D.S.B. setup.

Compatibility: They don't sting other corals with their tentacles, but they can produce toxic mucus which can affect corals it comes into contact with or that may be downcurrent from them.

Placement: They can be placed practically anywhere the current isn't too strong, but I suggest you try to keep them from coming into direct contact with other corals.

Just remember how big they can get, regardless of the size they are at the time of purchase.

Reproduction/Propagation: They can be cut in a number of ways as a means of propagation. They also regularly reproduce on their own through fission, forming small colonies.

Hardiness: If fed regularly, they are typically very hardy and able to adapt to a broad range of aquarium conditions.

Other Info: They can eat your fishes! They don't have much of a sting at all, but they feed by closing up around prey in a drawstring fashion. They sit partially closed, like a basket, then close up if anything swims in. This can be fun to watch if you want to supply them with small fishes for dinner.

Ricordea Mushrooms

Ricordea spp.

Description: *Ricordea* mushrooms are similar in overall appearance to other mushrooms and come in a wide range of colors and patterns, which include brown, orange, pink, and green. They are also often found in colonies attached to hard substrates. They often reach a full size of less than 2 inches. Their upper surfaces are covered by numerous rounded, bulb-like tentacles that set them apart from other mushrooms, too.

Lighting: They can be kept under a broad range of lighting, from low to high intensity, but most prefer low to moderate intensity.

Current: They prefer low current and will be folded over and unhappy in anything much stronger.

Feeding: They'll take small meaty foods if hand-fed and will also benefit from additions of plankton-type foods and/or a D.S.B. setup.

Compatibility: Many can burn other corals they come into contact with, although depending on what they come up against, they may also be injured by the stings of other corals.

Placement: They can be positioned about anywhere the current isn't too strong but should not be allowed to come into direct contact with other corals.

Reproduction/Propagation: They can be cut in a

Part 4

number of ways as a means of propagation. They also reproduce occasionally on their own through fission to form colonies.

Hardiness: These are relatively hardy as far as most corals go, but they are also typically the least hardy of the mushrooms.

Xenia (also called Pulse Corals, Pom-Pom Corals)
Xenia spp. and *Anthelia* spp.

Description: *Xenia* is an encrusting or stalked soft coral with relatively large pinnate polyps. The general form is a rubbery base/mat or trunk/stalk from which the 2- to 5-inch polyps emerge, and the colonies are typically "clump-like" in appearance.

Members of the genus *Anthelia* have long, highly pinnate tentacles that look like beautiful feathers and are easily confused with clove polyps. They form encrusting mats and typically come in shades of gray, cream, or light brown. Conversely, varieties of *Xenia* have trunks/stalks (and look like pom-poms) and often have tentacles that aren't as feather-like. They typically come in gray, cream, or white, and the polyps are commonly relatively short compared to those of *Anthelia* (although both do have polyps that are variable in length and character).

Lighting: They can usually be kept under moderate to high intensity lighting, but the brighter the better.

Current: *Xenia* corals prefer a strong, turbulent current, but can do fine in areas with moderate currents, too.

Feeding: Varieties of *Xenia* have greatly reduced digestive structures, and while they may eat at times, they do not seem to be reliant on food to any degree. They won't take anything you can hand-feed them either, so no food is necessary. They can still grow like crazy anyway.

Compatibility: They don't sting, but some types of *Xenia* exude toxins that are very detrimental to a number of stony corals. They do not need to come into contact with them for the toxins to cause problems, either. Thus, *Xenia* and many stony corals cannot be kept together at times. While this is true, successful cohabitation really depends on the species of each involved and the type(s) of filtration used on the tanks, etc. Many hobbyists have been very successful keeping both, but it may indeed take some trial and error to get there. Keep in mind that, like many other encrustors, these may grow right up to other corals and

Part 4

may overtake them. For this reason, give them some room.

Placement: They can be placed anywhere that the current and lighting are acceptable, but they need to be given space to grow.

Reproduction/Propagation: *Xenia* is easy to propagate a number of ways, including the cutting of colonies. Colonies also grow very quickly under optimal conditions and can spread over large areas of substrate and glass.

Hardiness: Hardiness is a tough question with several answers when it comes to *Xenia*. Many specimens fare very poorly during shipping and literally fall apart. However, if they survive and become acclimated to aquarium life, they can be exceptionally hardy and grow rapidly. However, for unknown reasons, every once in a while perfectly healthy *Xenia* may completely "crash," and whole colonies go limp and die in a short period of time. Several possible explanations for this occurrence (and preventatives) have been suggested, but none proven. Basically, you just have to hope for the best.

Other Info: Many varieties of *Xenia* and a few of *Anthelia* also have an unusual trait: a pumping or pulsing action. The polyps very actively and rhythmically open and close as if they were vigorously feeding (they aren't). Varieties of *Xenia* eat very little if any food, and they rely heavily on the absorption of nutrients directly from the surrounding water. It has been suggested that this pumping action helps to increase water flow over the polyps. This hasn't been proven either, and the notion is quite suspect considering that many varieties do not pulse but seem to have no problems growing and reproducing. The only thing known for sure is that they have a habit of stopping the pumping action when placed in aquariums, again for unknown reasons. Some colonies (even of the same species) will pump forever, while others may stop immediately and never start again. Frustrating!

Sea Mats (also called Colonial Anemones or Zoanthids)

Zoanthus spp.
Description: Sea mats are colonies of relatively small polyps, which are typically only a 1/2 inch or less in diameter and very short. However, the colonies can be very large, growing as encrusting mats from which the tightly spaced polyps emerge. Each polyp is ringed with numerous tiny tentacles and has an almost nonexistent mouth, and they typically come in brown, green, blue, or gray with lighter-colored centers. There are also occasional specimens that may be bright red or orange. They are found encrusted over a wide variety of surfaces, including other corals, but may also occasionally be seen partially buried in sand.

Lighting: They are heavily dependent on lighting and will need high-intensity illumination to thrive.

Part 4

Current: They prefer a moderate to strong current.

Feeding: Sea mats won't take foods you offer but still may benefit from plankton-type foods or a D.S.B. setup. Regardless, they can multiply rapidly as long as the lighting is sufficient.

Compatibility: They don't sting other corals but may overgrow them at times. They are susceptible to stings from more aggressive corals, though.

Placement: They can be placed any-where that the current and lighting are acceptable, and they won't be bothered by more aggressive corals.

Reproduction/Propagation: They are easy to propagate in a number of ways, including the cutting of mats. They also grow very quickly under optimal conditions and can spread over large areas of substrate, forming sizable colonies.

Hardiness: Provided with a good environment, they can be exceptionally hardy.

Other Info: They aren't really anemones; they just look a lot like them.

Button Polyps (also called Colonial Anemones or Palythoans)

Palythoa spp. and *Protopalythoa* spp.

Description: Button polyps are colonies of polyps that come in a couple of basic forms and range from about 1/2 inch to over 1 inch in diameter. Many form some sort of encrusting mats or bases, but there are some that can live as solitary polyps. These often end up forming colonies over time.

Members of the genus *Palythoa* form thick, encrusting, clump-like bases in which the polyps are embedded, with only the tops actually raising out of them. They are typically spaced closely enough for them to all touch and can close up into the base. Most are mixtures of brown, red, and/or cream, and their tentacles are so short they look more like a ring of bumps around their margins.

Conversely, members of the genus *Protopalythoa* have much taller polyps and no massive base like that of *Palythoa*. However, they are typically connected at the bottom of their stalks or by thin strips of flesh called "stolon." They also have larg-er tentacles, but they are still typically very short. Common colors are solid brown and red, but many are also mottled with cream, white, and/or green, and/or have cream or white stalks and bases.

Part 4

Lighting: They can live under a wide range of lighting conditions, but in general, the brighter the lights the better.

Current: Button polyps can live in a wide range of currents. Those that are deeply embedded in mats can tolerate very strong currents, while others that are taller will fare better in low to moderate currents.

Feeding: They'll eat small meaty foods provided by hand and will also benefit from additions of plankton-type foods and/or a D.S.B. setup.

Compatibility: They don't sting other corals, but they may overgrow them at times. They are susceptible to stings from more aggressive corals.

Placement: They can be placed anywhere that the current and lighting are acceptable, and other corals won't sting them.

Reproduction/Propagation: They are easy to propagate a number of ways, including the cutting of mats or severing of single polyps. They can also grow quickly under optimal conditions, forming large colonies.

Hardiness: Provided with a good environment, they can be exceptionally hardy.

Other Info: Button polyps aren't really anemones; they just look a lot like them. Actually, though, they are a type of zoanthid. However, they look fairly different due to their sizes and structures, so aquarists typically consider them to be separate from sea mats.

Also, many are known to produce exceptionally powerful toxins. These aren't a problem for other corals and such, but they kill fishes and possibly even humans. As is the case with many such corals, they don't seem to affect most people, but there are exceptions. Many people have reported having hallucinations, so wear gloves if you are going to handle them.

Yellow Polyps

Parazoanthus spp. (formerly *Parazoanthus gracilis*)
Description: Yellow polyps often form colonies or clusters, but they are usually either not actually attached to each other or are only joined by thin strips of flesh called "stolons." Their bodies/stalks are typically less than 1/4 inch in diameter, but they can be over 1 inch tall and have relatively long tentacles. They are found on

Part 4

hard substrates, but they are also often found living on other organisms, such as sponges. Of course, they are typically yellow in color.

Lighting: They can live under a wide range of lighting conditions, but in general, the brighter the lights the better.

Current: They prefer a low to moderate current.

Feeding: They'll greedily eat small meaty foods provided by hand and will also benefit from additions of plankton-type foods and/or a D.S.B. setup.

Compatibility: They can sting, produce toxins, and may actually kill stony corals they come into contact with. They are also susceptible to stings from more aggressive corals.

Placement: They can be placed anywhere that the current and lighting are acceptable but should be given some room where they won't sting or be stung by other corals.

Reproduction/Propagation: They are easy to propagate by allowing a few to grow onto a movable piece of substrate. They can also grow quickly under optimal conditions, forming large colonies.

Hardiness: Provided with a good environment, they can be exceptionally hardy. However, those that live in association with other organisms often rely on those organisms in some way and will die if they die. For example, if you should happen to buy any yellow polyps that are living in or on a sponge and the sponge dies, then the polyps will typically follow suit. It's better to stick with other specimens.

Other Info: Yellow polyps are also a type of zoanthid, but again, they have a unique appearance. Thus, they are typically considered as being separate from sea mats by aquarists. Also note that there are some species of *Parazoanthus* that are nonsymbiotic and will rely on food. Fortunately, these are uncommon in the hobby.

Star Polyps

Pachyclavularia violacea (formerly *Clavularia viridis*)
Description: Star polyps are small polyps that form rubber-like encrusting mats that they can retract into completely. These purple to reddish mats can cover about

Part 4

any surface and often grow right up the glass in aquariums. The polyps are most often bright fluorescent green but may also be cream. In addition, they have eight thin, finely pinnate tentacles. They also often have a lighter colored center, making the whole package quite beautiful.

Lighting: They can live under a wide range of lighting conditions, but in general, the brighter the lights the better.

Current: They can also live in a wide range of currents, but prefer low to moderate.

Feeding: Star polyps aren't going to take any food you try to give them, and they may not derive any benefit from plankton-type foods or a D.S.B. setup either. They'll grow just fine anyway.

Compatibility: They are resistant to the stings of most corals and can grow over almost anything. However, they are also susceptible to the stings of more aggressive varieties.

Placement: They can be placed anywhere that conditions are acceptable, which is just about anywhere, but they should be given some room where they won't overgrow or be stung by other corals.

Reproduction/Propagation: They are easy to propagate by the cutting of their mats and/or by allowing a few to grow onto a movable piece of substrate.

Hardiness: They are exceptionally hardy and rarely experience any problems if conditions are acceptable.

Clove Polyps (also called Daisy Polyps)

Clavularia spp.
Description: Clove polyps are colonial encrustors with long, thin stalks, most of which form small, clump-like bases or mats from which the polyps emerge. Others species can also grow as intermeshed networks of polyps that are joined only by thin strips of flesh called "stolons." The base and stolon material is quite tough and gives rise to short tubes that the polyps live in and can retract into. They cannot retract all the way down into the base, though. The polyps are quite fancy, as they have highly pinnate tentacles and look almost like feathers. They are typically yellowish, brown,

Part 4

green, or cream, with gray or cream bases and stolons.

Lighting: They can tolerate a broad range of lighting but will only thrive under moderate to bright illumination.

Current: Moderate currents are best, as strong currents will keep them from fully extending their delicate polyps.

Feeding: They aren't going to take any food you try to give them, and they may not derive any benefit from plankton-type foods or a D.S.B. setup either. They'll be fine despite this, as long as the lighting is acceptable.

Compatibility: They are highly resistant to the stings of almost all corals and can grow over almost anything.

Placement: They can be placed anywhere that conditions are acceptable, which is just about anywhere, but keep in mind that they can overrun other corals.

Reproduction/Propagation: They are easy to propagate by the cutting of their mats and/or by allowing a few to grow onto a movable piece of substrate.

Hardiness: They can be very hardy if kept under good conditions.

Colt Corals

Alcyonium spp., *Klyxum* spp., *Cladiella* spp., and others

Description: Colt corals are actually a number of very large, soft corals, typically having a single large base that immediately gives rise to several large branches. The branches are covered at their ends by retractable polyps which are highly pinnate, very feathery, and are typically pink, cream, or fleshy in color. The trunk and branches are usually much lighter in color, often being very light gray to almost white. They are quite a bit softer in consistency than other soft corals that are considered to be "leather" corals and are quite slimy to the touch.

Lighting: They can live under a wide range of lighting conditions, but in general, the brighter the lights the better, as long as you have plenty of room for them. If you don't, you'd better keep them under lower intensity lighting.

Current: As soft as they feel, colts will prefer a moderate to strong, turbulent current that helps to keep them upright and swaying around. They can do fine in areas with more moderate currents.

Feeding: They aren't going to take any food you try to give them and may not derive any benefit from many plankton-type foods or a D.S.B. setup either, as they feed on phytoplankton. They have no problem quickly growing to large sizes under good lighting with no food being added.

Compatibility: They shouldn't be any trouble to their neighbors, but they may be stung by some aggressive stony corals.

Placement: They can be placed anywhere that current and lighting are suitable, as well as anywhere they'll have plenty of room to grow.

Reproduction/Propagation: Colt corals are exceptionally easy to propagate, as they can be cut any way you choose. Small or large cuttings can grow into full-size specimens quickly. They can also reproduce on their own through fission, because the trunk can split in two.

Hardiness: They are exceptionally hardy and rarely experience any problems if conditions are acceptable.

Finger Leather Corals

Alcyonium spp., *Cladiella* spp., *Lobophytum* spp., and *Sinularia* spp.

Description: The name "finger leather coral" covers a number of genera and species that look similar and

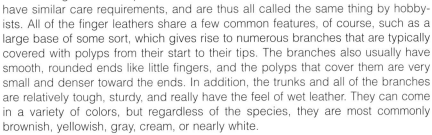

have similar care requirements, and are thus all called the same thing by hobbyists. All of the finger leathers share a few common features, of course, such as a large base of some sort, which gives rise to numerous branches that are typically covered with polyps from their start to their tips. The branches also usually have smooth, rounded ends like little fingers, and the polyps that cover them are very small and denser toward the ends. In addition, the trunks and all of the branches are relatively tough, sturdy, and really have the feel of wet leather. They can come in a variety of colors, but regardless of the species, they are most commonly brownish, yellowish, gray, cream, or nearly white.

Lighting: They can live under low to high intensity lighting, but most will grow very large very quickly under high intensity illumination.

Current: Finger leathers will do best with a moderate current but can often tolerate a higher or lower flow.

Feeding: They won't eat any food you give them and may not derive any benefit from many plankton-type foods or a D.S.B. setup either. Some may feed on phytoplankton, but they will typically grow to large sizes under good lighting with no food being added anyway.

Compatibility: Many soft corals can produce potent toxins, and some of the finger leathers are no exception. A few *Lobophyton* are considered to be some of the most

Part 4

toxic of all corals, and they can strongly affect stony corals anywhere near them. However, a few other finger leathers, like *Cladiella,* are perfectly safe. The best thing to do is not take any chances and assume that what you have can be toxic and may affect others, requiring a specimen to be moved. Conversely, many of them can also be stung by aggressive stony corals, too.

Placement: They can be placed anywhere that the current and lighting are suitable, as well as anywhere they'll have plenty of room to grow.

Reproduction/Propagation: Finger leathers are easy to propagate, as they can be cut any way you like, and the cuttings can grow into full-size specimens quickly. They can also reproduce on their own through fission, as the trunk can split in two, and through auto-fragmentation.

Hardiness: They are typically very hardy and rarely experience any problems if kept under acceptable conditions.

Other Info: Finger leathers will sometimes retract their polyps and cover themselves with a shiny sheet that should peel off in a few days. This is normal, as it is a means of clearing the upper surface of algal growth and sediments. The sheet can be toxic to many other corals, though, so try to collect it as it sloughs away, before it lands on an unlucky victim.

Tree Leather Corals

Capnella **spp.,** *Lemnalia* **spp.,** *Litophyton* **spp., and** *Nepthea* **spp.,**
Description: The name "tree leather coral" covers several genera and species that look relatively similar and have similar care requirements. They share a few common features, such as a large base of some sort, which gives rise to numerous thin branches that are covered with rather bushy polyps. These bushy polyps aren't as small as those of a finger leather but are much smaller and less fancy than those of a colt coral. The branches also lack the smooth, rounded ends like those of a finger leather coral. However, they do have the characteristically leather-like toughness, although they may have a slicker, slimier surface than other leathers. They can come in a variety of colors, but regardless of the species, they are most commonly brownish, greenish, pinkish, cream, or nearly white.

Lighting: Most can live under a wide range of lighting conditions but will do best under moderate to strong illumination. However, some members of the genus *Nepthea* are nonsymbiotic and can live under any lighting conditions.

Part 4

Current: They fare best with a turbulent current that is moderate to strong.

Feeding: They won't eat any food you give them, but all will likely require the use of plankton-type foods and/or a D.S.B. setup. This is especially true for *Capnella* and *Nepthea*. In fact, because many *Nepthea* are nonsymbiotic, they won't last long at all without a constant supply of particulate/plankton foods.

Compatibility: With the exception of *Capnella*, all of these can produce potent toxins that may have strong effects on nearby corals depending on the species of each involved and the type(s) of filtration used in the tanks. Many corals may be affected no matter what you do, requiring the relocation of a specimen. To the contrary, sometimes they seem to have no effect on anything and cause no problems whatsoever, but may be stung by aggressive stony corals instead, as is usually the case with *Capnella*.

Placement: They can be placed anywhere that current and lighting are suitable.

Reproduction/Propagation: They can be easy to propagate because they can be cut any way you choose. Cuttings can grow into full-size specimens, albeit more slowly than many other leather corals. They can also reproduce on their own through auto-fragmentation and fission, as their trunks can split in two.

Hardiness: Many of these corals do not fare well during shipping. They are also more difficult to care for than other leather corals due to their food needs. They are slower growing than other leather corals, and on top of all that, they have an unexplainable habit of occasionally going limp, falling over, and literally dropping dead without warning. I suggest you stick to something else.

Cabbage Leather Corals (also called Lettuce Corals)

Sinularia spp.

Description: Cabbage leather corals look quite different, as they are short and leafy instead of tall and branched. They also have very few small polyps. In fact, sometimes the polyps are only found sprouting out here and there along the edges of the "leaves" and nowhere else. Generally, they are found in shades of brown or green, or are grayish, and they do have the characteristic leathery feel that other leather corals share.

Lighting: They can live under a wide range of lighting conditions, but in general, the brighter the lights the better.

Current: They thrive in areas where the current is moderate to strong.

Feeding: They rely on lighting and the absorption of nutrients, so there's no need to feed them.

Compatibility: Cabbages don't sting, but they may produce relatively potent toxins

Part 4

in enough quantity to have strong effects on some stony corals depending on the type(s) of filtration used in the tanks. Some corals placed nearby may be strongly affected, but in many cases they seem to have no effect on other corals and don't cause any problems at all.

Placement: They can be placed anywhere that current and lighting are suitable.

Reproduction/Propagation: Like other leather corals, they are exceptionally easy to propagate, as they can be cut any way you like. They can also reproduce on their own through fission and auto-fragmentation.

Hardiness: They are exceptionally hardy and rarely experience any problems if conditions are acceptable.

Toadstool Leather Corals (also called Umbrella Leather Corals)

Sarcophyton spp.

Description: Toadstool leather corals are a long-time favorite and one of the most popular corals around. They look like big toadstools, with a typically rounded, dome-shaped cap that sits upon a rounded stalk/trunk. Colonies are usually cream, brown, yellow, or pink, and while the stalks are smooth, numerous slender polyps with fine, pinnate tentacles cover the upper sides of the caps. These polyps are variable in length and form, and they often have light-colored tips.

Colonies can reach sizes over 2 feet in diameter, and they don't always have a nice stalk and round cap. In fact, many may have no stalk and look like a cap stuck directly onto a hard substrate, while others may have a cap that looks more like a big ruffled punchbowl. Still others may have large knobs or folds on their caps.

Lighting: They can live under a wide range of lighting conditions, but in general, the brighter the lights the better—if you have a big tank. If you want to intentionally keep them from getting huge, keep them under lower intensity lighting.

Current: They thrive in moderate currents and won't polyp-out in currents that are too strong. They also won't do very well in areas where the flow is too slow, allowing sediment to collect on top of them.

Feeding: They rely on lighting and the absorption of nutrients, so there's no need to feed them.

Compatibility: They don't sting, but they can produce large amounts of relatively potent toxins, which may have strong effects on stony corals depending on the species of each involved and the type(s) of filtration used in the tanks. Many corals placed downstream from toadstools may be affected no matter what you try, requiring someone to be relocated. With that said, in many other cases, they seem to have no effect on anything and cause no problems whatsoever.

Placement: They can be placed anywhere that current and lighting are suitable.

Reproduction/Propagation: Leather corals of all sorts are exceptionally easy to propagate, as they can be cut any way you choose. Even very small cuttings can grow into large specimens quickly. Toadstools can also reproduce on their own through fission, auto-fragmentation, and budding.

Hardiness: They are exceptionally hardy and rarely experience any problems if conditions are acceptable.

Other Info: The nightly retraction of the polyps is normal, and they may even stay retracted during the day at times. This is nothing to worry about unless they stay retracted for more than a couple of days. Also, they will sometimes retract their polyps and cover themselves with a shiny sheet, which should peel off in a few days. This is normal, too, as it is a means of clearing the upper surface of algal growth and sediments. The scraps from the sheet can be toxic to many other corals, though, so try to collect it as it peels off, before it lands on a neighbor.

Gorgonians (also called Sea Rods, Whips, Plumes, or Fans)

Many genera

Description: Gorgonians are a diverse group of large corals that can take on a number of forms, but they all share some basic features. First, they all have a tough proteinaceous internal skeleton that is typically nothing more than a thin branching rod wrapped in fleshy tissue. They are also covered by numerous pinnate polyps that emerge from the branches, many of which can retract completely inside the tissue at will.

The members of one group are commonly known as sea rods (ex. *Eunicea* spp., *Muricea* spp., *Plexaura* spp., *Pseudoplexaura* spp.), all of which have simple, relatively thick branches and large polyps. They are highly variable in color, but the majority of them have grayish-brown or orange-brown branches and dark-colored polyps. However, there are a few types (ex. *Swiftia* spp. and *Diodogorgia* spp.) that are nonsymbiotic and always come in much brighter colors, such as red, orange, yellow, and purple, with white or clear polyps.

Part 4

The sea whips are the next group (ex. *Pterogorgia* spp.), and they have compressed/flattened branches with smaller polyps that extend only from the sides/edges of the branches instead of all over. They are most commonly brown, gray, or purple, and many have light-colored polyps, rather than dark ones.

Sea plumes are the next bunch (ex. *Pseudopterogorgia* spp.), all of which have a long central branch with numerous closely spaced branches coming from it, making the whole thing look like a giant feather. I say giant because these get BIG, as in taller than a person! They almost always come in purple and have tightly spaced, light-colored polyps.

Lastly, we get to the sea fans (ex. *Gorgonia* spp.), which are far more commonly seen in shell shops than aquarium shops. These really look like big fans and have a flat, mesh-like structure that is quite unique. They are often sold as dried out, dark-brown curios. When alive and covered in flesh, they are typically purple or gray, with some being yellow or other lighter colors, as well, and have small, dark polyps that emerge from the inside surfaces of the intertwined branches.

Lighting: All symbiotic gorgonians can thrive under moderate to high intensity lighting, typically the brighter the better. Those that are nonsymbiotic obviously need no light, but they can also tolerate bright illumination (although this often leads to the growth of algae on them).

Current: Gorgonians will need moderate to strong currents and will do best with a turbulent flow that makes them sway back and forth and around. Sea fans in particular will require strong currents that hit them alternately from both sides, perpendicular to their flat feeding surfaces. Due to their unusual form, non-perpendicular flow won't do them much good.

Feeding: Many eat small meaty foods provided by hand and will also benefit from additions of plankton-type foods and/or a D.S.B. setup. You may have to experiment a bit, though, as there are a few that eat phytoplankton only.

Compatibility: Most gorgonians can produce toxins, but these rarely pose a problem in aquariums, as they are made to deter predators rather than to poison neighbors. A few can produce very short sweeper tentacles and may sting corals they come in contact with, but some other corals can also sting them, too.

Part 4

Placement: Gorgonians can be placed anywhere that current and lighting are acceptable, as well as anywhere they won't brush against other corals.

Reproduction/Propagation: Most gorgonians can be propagated quite easily by cutting off pieces of various sizes from the ends of their branches. However, this often doesn't work very well for sea fans due to their structure. Many can also reproduce on their own by dropping off little pieces of branches themselves, which can attach to hard substrates and form new corals.

Hardiness: Relatively thick-branched, large-polyped, symbiotic sea rods and sea plumes are typically very hardy and seldom have any problems if conditions are acceptable. However, nonsymbiotic species very rarely survive long-term. Due to their forms, current requirements, etc., the sea whips and fans also have poor survival records, with sea fans in particular being nearly impossible to keep long-term as best as I know.

Due to their well-documented, exceptionally poor survival records in captivity, I advise you to stay away from all sea fans and nonsymbiotic gorgonians. Because sea whips often don't fare significantly better, I also recommend that you stick to the symbiotic sea rods and plumes only.

Encrusting Gorgonians (also called Corky Sea Fingers)

Briareum asbestinium and *Briareum stechei*
Description: Unlike "regular" gorgonians, these are encrustors that grow over surfaces. They can form flattened mats over rocks and such, which may send up branches, but they can also grow over other corals, especially other living gorgonians. Thus, they can take on the forms of anything they grow over. Their thick, fleshy rinds are typically purple or gray, and they have large pinnate polyps that are usually brown or greenish.

Lighting: They can thrive under moderate to high intensity lighting, typically the brighter the better.

Current: They need moderate to strong currents to thrive.

Feeding: These depend on their zooxanthellae and the collection of particulate matter, thus they won't need anything you can provide for them. They seem to do just fine anyway.

Compatibility: Encrusting gorgonians can produce several toxins, but these won't be a problem because they are made to deter predators rather than to poison neighbors. However, they are highly resistant to the defenses of many other corals and can grow right over them at times. As a result, you should be more worried about everything else.

Part 4

Placement: You can put them anywhere that current and lighting are acceptable, but make sure to give them plenty of room to grow. Once they get going, they are essentially impossible to stop!

Reproduction/Propagation: These can be propagated very easily by cutting off pieces of various sizes from the ends of their branches or from anywhere you can make a cut on an encrusting colony.

Hardiness: Encrusting gorgonians are typically very hardy and seldom have any problems if conditions are acceptable.

Other Info: Like some other soft corals, these can produce and shed mucous sheets to clean themselves off. Thus, if you find that a specimen is encased, don't fret. The sheet should come off by itself.

Stony Corals

Stony corals are best defined as any species of coral that produces an external calcium-based skeleton. Some are more "stony" than others and these corals are often responsible for the primary reef-building operations throughout the tropics. Much of the live rock that you may have purchased for your reef aquarium was once a colony of stony corals.

Stony Corals are primarily responsible for the reef-building operations in the tropics.

Plate Corals (also called Disc Corals)

Fungia spp. and many less common genera

Description: Plate corals are relatively large free-living corals that are typically disc-like or dome-shaped in form, with very short or no tentacles. They can be found in a broad range of colorations, from solid pink to mottled blue and cream. Although they may be attached to a substrate when small, plate corals eventually break free from their own weight as they grow, and eventually become free-living adults.

Lighting: Plates can thrive under moderate to high intensity lighting.

Current: Low to moderate. If it's too strong, a plate's soft tissues will stay retracted in the grooves in its skeleton.

Feeding: Plates will eat small meaty foods provided by hand and will also benefit from additions of invertebrate foods and/or a D.S.B. setup.

Compatibility: They typically don't cause any trouble, but may smother adjacent corals with mucus if they get too close and become irritated.

Placement: Plates should be placed flat on the bottom, preferably on a soft substrate if they are dome-shaped and can easily keep themselves cleared of sediment, or on rubble if they are flatter in form and cannot.

Reproduction/Propagation: Because they are solitary corals, they are not propagated. However, they have been known to reproduce on their own at times through the production of anthocauli and/or polyp buds.

Hardiness: They are often injured during collection or transport due to the presence of sharp, raised septa but typically do very well once acclimated if they recover from any such injuries.

Other Info: Plates can tolerate a fairly wide range of lighting and current conditions, but believe it or not, they have been known to move themselves when "unhappy" with their placement in an aquarium. To do this, they bloat their tissues with water, and then through the use of subtle muscular contractions, manage to slowly creep across surfaces. Hobbyists have reported that when given the opportunity they can even move up inclined surfaces until they are "happy." This can be quite a surprise considering their appearance, but it is only a problem in cases when they literally dump large amounts of toxic mucus upon other corals with which they may come into contact.

Long-Tentacle Plate Corals (also called Long-Tentacle Disc Corals)

Heliofungia actiniformis

Description: Long-tentacle plate corals are relatively large, free-living corals that have flattened disc-like forms. They are free-living as adults; however, they may be attached to a hard substrate when small, in which cases they eventually break free from their own weight as they grow. Unlike the numerous species of plate corals with short or no tentacles, long-tentacle plate corals are all the same species (so far) and possess tentacles that are so long that they look far more like sea anemones than stony corals. Ironically, when the tentacles are completely retracted, they look almost identical to that of a short-tentacle plate coral. As far as coloration goes, these corals are typically brown or green with light-colored tentacle tips. They also typically have contrasting light-colored stripes on the body.

Lighting: They need moderate to high intensity lighting. While they can thrive in a range of lighting conditions, they typically require more intense lighting than other plates and also depend more on feeding for success.

Current: Low to moderate. If it's too strong, a plate's soft tissues and tentacles will stay retracted in the grooves in its skeleton.

Feeding: They will eat small meaty foods provided by hand and will also benefit from additions of invertebrate foods and/or a D.S.B. setup.

Compatibility: Because the tentacles are so long and loaded with stinging cells, these corals must be treated with respect. They need LOTS of room because the tentacles can be used as lethal weapons against neighboring corals, even if they are several inches away. As a result, be careful where you put one!

Placement: They should be placed flat on the bottom, preferably on soft substrate or rubble, well away from other corals.

Reproduction/Propagation: Because they are single polyps, they are not propagated, but they may reproduce by themselves through the production of polyp buds.

Hardiness: They are often injured during collection/transport due to the presence of sharp, raised septa but typically do very well once acclimated if they recover from any such injuries.

Part 4

Tooth Corals (also called Doughnut or Button Corals)

Cynarina lacrymalis and *Scolymia vitiensis*

Description: Tooth corals are relatively large, rounded, solitary corals that have a small skeleton and lots of soft tissue. The skeleton is often only a couple of inches across and ringed by large, teeth-like septa with jagged tops (hence the tooth name), but when a specimen is fully expanded, it may easily reach a diameter of 8 inches or more. They are most commonly found attached to hard substrates on walls and overhangs and other surfaces, but may at times be found unattached and living on a soft bottom.

Like those of many other corals, their mouths will pucker up and open when food is nearby. The detection of food also brings out a ring of hidden feeding tentacles that are extended to capture prey at night and are normally kept under a flap/ring of tissue that surrounds the mouth during the day. In aquariums, though, if food is given, they'll come out regardless of the time.

Cynarina has a single mouth and comes in a wide variety of colors, but most are commonly red or mottled red with some other color, such as green. The tissue that makes up the body is very thin and translucent, and when it is expanded you can actually see the skeleton with all of its teeth inside.

Oddly enough, *Scolymia* may have more than one mouth, despite the fact that they are single polyps. They also come in a variety of colors but are most commonly red or green; they are often mottled or covered by cream-colored spots, blotches, or stripes. Also, while the tissues of *Cynarina* are smooth, billowy, and translucent, swelling up and out, those of *Scolymia* are much heavier, relatively opaque and rough looking, and swell laterally far more than upward.

Lighting: Tooth corals prefer low to moderate intensity lighting and often will not fully expand under anything brighter.

Current: Because they have such large, soft bodies, they will not expand in strong currents. They prefer low currents in which they can really swell without risk of being damaged by their own skeleton or their surroundings.

Feeding: They'll take meaty foods of a variety of sizes, from brine shrimp to very small fishes if hand-fed and may also benefit from additions of invertebrate foods and/or a D.S.B. setup.

Compatibility: Tooth corals have feeding tentacles, but they are so small relative to the size of the body that they shouldn't be considered a threat to anything else. Conversely, they are very susceptible to stings from more dangerous corals and are thought to be more strongly affected by toxins given off by neighbors.

Placement: They can be placed successfully in just about any area where the lighting and current are suitable and they have plenty of room to expand fully. Just keep in mind that they'll be much bigger when swollen and may extend into the range of other corals or into areas of higher than desired flow.

Reproduction/Propagation: Because they are single polyps, they are not propagated, and I don't know of any cases of them reproducing by themselves.

Hardiness: Unfortunately, the long-term survival record of tooth corals is highly variable. Some seem to last forever with little attention, while others perish in even the best of conditions. The exact reason(s) for this disparity is unknown, but it is there nonetheless. In short, don't be too heartbroken if you choose to try one and it doesn't make it when more durable corals do.

Open Brain Corals

Trachyphyllia geoffroyi and the "ex" *Wellsophyllia radiata*

Description: Open brain corals are relatively small, free-living corals (although some do live attached to a hard substrate when small) that range in form from flattened cones, to flabello-meandroid, to domed. However, the most common form by far is the flabello-meandroid. All develop multiple mouths as they grow; they also possess numerous hidden, very small feeding tentacles that typically stay out of sight under a flap during the day but come out day or night when food is provided.

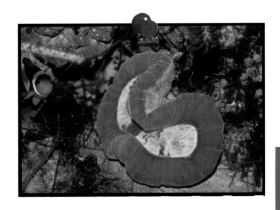

Flabello-meandroid specimens have a small, cone-shaped base (as do the cone-shaped forms, of course), while those that are domed have a flat-bottomed skeleton, and almost all specimens come in various mixes of green and red. Some may be bluish or gray, but these are far less common. As is the case with many fleshy corals, they may also expand to a surprising size well beyond the boundaries of their skeletons.

Lighting: Open brain corals can tolerate a broad range of lighting, from low to high intensity.

Current: They prefer a low to moderate current, and they will not expand fully if currents are too strong.

Part 4

Feeding: Open brain corals will eat small meaty foods provided by hand and will also benefit from additions of invertebrate foods and/or a D.S.B. setup.

Compatibility: They have feeding tentacles, but they are so small relative to the size of the body that they shouldn't be considered a threat to anything else. They can, however, be very sensitive to stings from more dangerous corals.

Placement: Open brains will do best if placed on the bottom, on a soft sediment substrate, away from other possibly aggressive corals.

Reproduction/Propagation: Because of their form, they are not propagated, but they have been known to reproduce by themselves through the production of polyp buds.

Hardiness: Open brains are typically very hardy; however, on occasion they may begin to recede from their skeletons and/or stop expanding their tissues for unknown reasons. They often recover from such problems, but not always.

Other Info: For years, *Trachyphyllia geoffroyi* and *Wellsophyllia radiata* were thought to be different corals, as *T. geoffroyi* has a cone-shaped skeleton and *W. radiata* has a round, flat-bottomed skeleton. However, it has recently been discovered that both are actually different forms of the same species, and both are now called *T. geoffroyi*.

Elegance Corals

Catalaphyllia jardinei
Description: Elegance corals are very large, free-living corals (although some do live attached to a hard substrate when small) that range in form from flattened cones to flabello-meandroid, with the most common being an open flabello-mean-droid form. They develop multiple mouths as they grow, and also possess numerous very powerful feeding tentacles that can be in the neighborhood of a foot long and can capture live fish with no problems.

Coming in various mixes of bright fluorescent green, pink, cream, and purple, their bodies can swell well past the boundaries of their skeleton to huge sizes, and they can really take up a lot of room in an aquarium. In fact, I'd say that due to their size and the length and potency of their tentacles, a full-grown specimen will require more room than any other coral I can think of.

Lighting: Elegance corals can live under a broad range of lighting conditions, from low to high intensity.

Current: They prefer low to moderate currents that allow them to fully expand their soft tissues.

Feeding: They'll need to be fed meaty food and may enjoy a variety of sizes, from

Part 4

brine shrimp to good-sized fishes. They will also benefit from the addition of invertebrate foods and/or a D.S.B. setup.

Compatibility: Elegance corals will sting and kill just about anything they come into contact with (although there are exceptions). However, it's possible that they are sensitive to substances given off by many soft corals.

Placement: Elegance corals live on soft bottoms in their natural habitat and should be placed accordingly in an aquarium, with their bases partially buried in the substrate.

Reproduction/Propagation: Due to their form, they are not propagated, but they have been known to reproduce by themselves through the production of polyp buds.

Hardiness: Here's the bad part. For unknown reasons, elegance corals just aren't what they used to be. Many years ago, specimens were nearly indestructible in my experience and were very desirable. Today, however, they often refuse to last no matter how well they are cared for. Many long-time hobbyists have noticed this and are left scratching their heads. While several possible reasons have been forwarded, all are speculative. For this reason, I have to say that you should stay away from this coral, even though they may seem to be in stores everywhere.

Other Info: Despite the problems, LOTS of hobbyists are apparently still buying this coral anyway—some out of ignorance, others out of stubbornness. This is obvious, because just about every coral-selling store I walk into regularly has them in stock.

Fox Corals

Nemezophyllia turbida
Description: Fox corals are moderate in size, with a thin, wall-like, flabello-meandroid skeleton that is topped by fairly large septa. The polyps are very unusual in that they expand a great deal, but there are no tentacles at all. In fact, when fully expanded, they can completely obscure the skeleton and look almost like clusters of mushroom anemones. Living attached to hard substrates, they come in green, cream, and brown.

Lighting: Foxes can thrive under low to moderate intensity lighting but will tolerate higher intensity lighting as well.

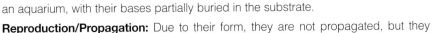

Part 4

Current: They enjoy low currents but will still expand significantly in moderate currents. They will not expand in strong currents, though.

Feeding: Foxes are not known to take any hand-fed foods, but they may benefit from additions of invertebrate foods and/or a D.S.B. setup.

Compatibility: They have no tentacles and are resistant to the stings of other corals. Thus, they are some of the most benign and peaceful of all corals.

Placement: Due to their peaceful nature, they can be placed about anywhere that lighting and current conditions are suitable.

Reproduction/Propagation: Fox corals are not propagated due to their form, and they have not been observed reproducing on their own in aquariums.

Hardiness: Fox corals have been consistently durable but may suffer from localized tissue recession at times. This condition typically doesn't spread far, and the corals often recover.

Lobo Brain Corals (also called Meat Corals)

Lobophyllia hemiprichii and a few others

Description: Lobo brains are rather large corals with heavy skeletons coming in flabello-meandroid, domed, or branched forms. All have thick, fleshy polyps with rough surfaces, and they are available in a very wide range of colors and patterns, from solid green, orange, purple, and red, to mottled mixtures of even more hues. The skeleton is always firmly attached to a hard substrate, and when they are branching in form, the polyps only occupy the ends of the branches. They do have small feeding tentacles, but these typically stay out of sight under a flap/ring of tissue during the day. They are extended only at night or when food is provided in an aquarium.

Lighting: Lobo brains can be found in a wide variety of environments and can thrive under moderate to high intensity lighting. However, they also usually fare well under lower intensity lighting.

Current: They do well in a low to moderate current and won't fully expand their tissues if the current is too strong.

Feeding: Lobo brains will eat small meaty foods provided by hand and will also

Part 4

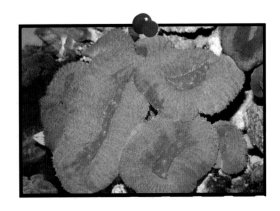

benefit from additions of invertebrate foods and/or a D.S.B. setup.

Compatibility: Their feeding tentacles are very short and should not be a problem for other corals. As a result, they are considered to be quite nonaggressive and are fairly resistant to the stings of other corals.

Placement: Because they are nonaggressive and can tolerate a wide range of lighting intensities and currents, they can be placed just about anywhere in an aquarium.

Reproduction/Propagation: Due to their forms, most are not propagated. However, those that have a branching skeleton can be broken or sawed apart very carefully. This will not affect the polyps living at the ends of the branches.

Hardiness: Lobos are consistently very durable and are an excellent choice, but they may suffer from tissue recession at times.

Bubble Corals

Plerogyra sinuosa and *Plerogyra simplex*
Description: Bubble corals are relatively moderate in size and are well known for having some of the most unusual tentacles of all the corals. Their skeletons are always attached to a hard substrate and can be round, flabello-meandroid, or branching in form, but the tentacles really stand out because they often look just like smooth bubbles. Others look even more odd, as their bubbles are covered with knobs (the octobubble form). On top of this, they also have huge, widely spaced, blade-like septa that make them clearly identifiable, even when the soft tissues are completely retracted.

In addition to the unique bubbles, they also have rather normal looking feeding tentacles that can reach out from between them, extending an inch or two at night (and sometimes during the day, too). They also have very long sweeper tentacles. Regardless of their form, all of them are cream, white, or green in color, and many have little details on the bubbles that are quite interesting. A few have a shimmering band down the middle of each bubble, while many others have bubbles with something of a fingerprint pattern covering them.

Telling the species apart is quite easy, as *P. sinuosa* isn't branched and *P. simplex* is.

Part 4

However, people are usually confused when they find out that the branching forms are *P. simplex*, while both the smooth bubble and knobby bubble varieties that don't branch are *P. sinuosa*. As different as the bubbles may appear, it has not yet been determined whether or not the octo-bubble form is a subspecies of *P. sinuosa* or a separate species altogether. At least for now, they are still considered the same despite their appearances.

Lighting: Bubbles can thrive under a broad range of lighting conditions, from what would be considered the absolute lowest intensity to the fullest intensity. However, they prefer low to moderate intensity, and specimens that were collected from dimmer areas are susceptible to light shock if illuminated too much. The bubbles are inflated and deflated to help control how much light the zooxanthellae receive, so those placed under lower intensity lighting will also typically increase the size of their bubbles.

Current: They will inflate their bubbles fully only in a lower current but can tolerate a moderate current. They will not expand at all in high current areas, as tearing or cutting by their own septa would certainly damage them.

Feeding: They'll eat a variety of meaty foods, from brine shrimp to very small fishes, and they will also benefit from additions of invertebrate foods and/or a D.S.B. setup.

Compatibility: Bubbles can reach out several inches with their slender sweeper tentacles, which are quite powerful. As a result, you'll need to be sure to give them plenty of room.

Placement: Areas with low current and low intensity lighting are best, and they are typically found attached to vertical walls and overhangs.

Reproduction/Propagation: They are not propagated due to their form, but they have been known to extend their flesh to nearby surfaces, which eventually forms a new coral in an odd form of polyp budding. Tissue often covers much of the skeleton, even in the branching form, so you probably shouldn't attempt to break or saw one apart either.

Hardiness: Bubbles can be very hardy, yet many fail within the first few weeks. Because they have such oversized and sharp septa, they are very prone to skele-

Part 4

tal damage and/or cuts. The key, then, is finding a specimen that has not been injured during collection and shipping. If you can find one that has no apparent injuries, the only other common malady is tissue recession. Tissue recession may be only localized and reversible, but other times it may overtake whole specimens.

Hammer Corals (also called Anchor Corals)

Euphyllia ancora and *Euphyllia parancora*

Description: Hammers are an all-time favorite and are one of the most common corals seen in the hobby. Colonies can grow quite large and have skeletons that are always attached, being flabello-meandroid *(E. ancora)* or branched *(E. parancora)*. They are all easy to identify because they have long tentacles terminated with hammer-like knobs that come in various shades of fluorescent green and brown, with lighter-colored tips. They also come in pinkish and bluish colors. You should also note that not only do these corals have long tentacles, but they can also develop sweeper tentacles that may even be three or four times longer.

Lighting: Hammers can tolerate a wide range of lighting but will fare best under moderate to high intensity illumination.

Current: They will expand best in low to moderate currents and will not expand at all in high current areas.

Feeding: Hammers will take meaty foods of a variety of sizes, from brine shrimp to small fishes, and will also benefit from additions of invertebrate foods and/or a D.S.B. setup.

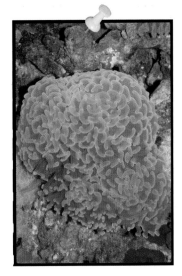

Compatibility: The tentacles are deadly by themselves, and then there are the extra-long sweepers. Hammers can quickly dispatch almost any other coral they come into contact with in a matter of hours.

Placement: They've got those long, strong tentacles, and they grow fast, too. This means, you'll need to give them plenty of room in an area with suitable lighting and currents.

Reproduction/Propagation: Non-branching forms are not propagated but may reproduce by producing polyp buds. Branching forms can be broken or sawed apart because the polyps reside at the ends of the branches. They can also produce polyp buds as well.

Hardiness: Hammers are hardy corals that often fare well if they survive the first few days or weeks in captivity. As is the case with many corals, they ship very poorly and often suffer from injuries, which commonly lead to brown jelly infections and death. As a result, you'll need to look closely and find a healthy specimen.

Other Info: As deadly as they may be, hammers and frogspawns can touch each other with no problems.

Frogspawn Corals (also called Octopus or Grape Corals)
Euphyllia divisa and *Euphyllia paradivisa*

Description: Frogspawns are a long-time favorite and are one of the most common corals seen in shops. Colonies can grow quite large and have skeletons that are always attached, being flabello-meandroid *(E. divisa)* or branched *(E. paradivisa)*, both of which are easy to identify because they have long tentacles terminated with knobby, wart-like bumps. The tentacles are sometimes clear but are usually various shades of fluorescent green and brown, and the tentacle bumps are lighter, sometimes being cream colored. They can also develop much longer sweeper tentacles that may be three or four times longer than the normal ones.

Lighting: They can tolerate a wide range of lighting but will fare best under moderate to high intensity illumination.

Current: Frogspawns will expand best in low to moderate currents and will not expand at all in high current areas.

Feeding: Frogspawns will take meaty foods of a variety of sizes, from brine shrimp to small fishes, and will also benefit from additions of invertebrate foods and/or a D.S.B. setup.

Compatibility: Their normal tentacles are quite deadly by themselves, and then there are the extended sweepers. Frogspawns can quickly kill almost any other coral they come into contact with in a matter of hours.

Placement: They have long, powerful sweeper tentacles, and they can grow fast. As a result, you'll need to give them lots of room in an area with suitable lighting and currents.

Reproduction/Propagation: Branching and non-branching forms can produce polyp buds. Non-branching forms are not propagated, but branching forms can be broken or sawed apart since the polyps reside at the ends of the branches.

Hardiness: Frogspawns are hardy corals that often fare well if they survive the first few days or weeks in captivity.

As is the case with many corals, they ship very poorly and often suffer from injuries, which commonly lead to brown jelly infections and death. Thus, you'll need to look closely and find a healthy specimen.

Other Info: As deadly as they may be, frogspawns and hammers can touch each other without injury.

Torch Corals

Euphyllia glabrescens

Description: Torch corals are also members of the genus *Euphyllia,* but they are only found in branching forms and lack the unusual sorts of tentacles that hammers and frogspawns have. They're typically fluorescent green or brownish, and the tentacles usually end with a little rounded tip that is lighter in color. In addition, they are always attached and branching in form.

Lighting: Torches can tolerate a wide range of lighting but will fare best under moderate to high intensity illumination.

Current: They will expand best in low to moderate currents and will not likely expand at all in high current areas.

Feeding: Torches will take meaty foods of a variety of sizes, from brine shrimp to very small fishes, and will also benefit from additions of invertebrate foods and/or a D.S.B. setup.

Compatibility: The tentacles of a torch coral don't seem to be as potent as those of their cousins, and they don't produce sweeper tentacles either. However, this does not mean they are not a threat to nearby corals that they may touch.

Placement: They can be placed anywhere that the current and lighting are suitable, and they don't need as much space as other corals that have longer sweeper tentacles. Nonetheless, they should be given at least a few inches of extra room to allow for future growth.

Reproduction/Propagation: They can be broken or sawed apart because the polyps only occupy the ends of the branches, and they have been known to produce polyp buds.

Part 4

Hardiness: Unfortunately, torch corals have not proven to be very hardy at all. There are occasional success stories, but I think that overall they have fared poorly, as they seem to be overly prone to suffer from recession and brown jelly infections. They also have a terrible time with collection and shipping, making it all the more difficult to find a good specimen.

Trumpet Corals (also called Candy Cane Corals)

Caulastrea furcata and *Caulastrea echinulata*

Description: These are typically relatively small colonial corals, with specimens comprised of a dozen or fewer polyps (but they can really grow quickly). The skeletons are always attached to a hard substrate and are branching in form, with the

polyps occupying only the ends of each branch. Specimens of *C. furcata* are more common and have doughnut-shaped polyps that are usually brown with light-colored green centers and sometimes with radiating white stripes where the underlying septa are located, while the polyps of *C. echinulata* are often more asymmetrical and solid gray. All have very small feeding tentacles that are retained under a ring/flap of tissue until nighttime or feeding time.

Lighting: Trumpets will thrive under moderate intensity lighting but will not fare as well under low or high intensity illumination.

Current: They will expand best with a moderate current but can live in lower currents. However, they often will not expand at all in areas with higher flow.

Feeding: Trumpets will take small meaty foods if hand-fed and will also benefit from additions of invertebrate foods and/or a D.S.B. setup.

Compatibility: Surprise! These innocent looking corals produce slender sweeper tentacles that can deliver a strong sting. Fortunately, they aren't very long and are able to reach out only a couple of inches at best.

Placement: They can be placed anywhere conditions are right, as long as you give them a minimum of a couple of inches of space to account for the reach of their sweepers.

Reproduction/Propagation: Because the polyps only occupy the ends of their lightweight branches, colonies can be broken or sawed apart with ease. Trumpets also grow quickly, making propagation well worth the effort.

Hardiness: If placed properly, trumpets tend to be very hardy and are a great choice.

Tongue Corals (also called Slipper Corals)

Herpolitha limax and *Polyphyllia talpina*

Description: Tongues are relatively large, free-living corals that have low, typically straight, elongated forms and very short tentacles. They are less commonly found in v-shaped or y-shaped forms and have been known to reach over 2 feet in length in aquariums. As they grow, both species develop multiple mouths, but to tell the two species apart, look for a prominent central groove that runs down the length of *H. limax,* which is absent for *P. talpina*. *Polyphyllia talpina* also typically has a greater number of longer tentacles (still less than an inch long, though), which have light-colored tips. Both are predominantly brownish, green, or cream in color.

Lighting: Tongue corals will thrive under moderate to high intensity lighting but may survive under lower intensity lighting.

Current: Low to moderate. If it's too strong, a tongue's soft tissues will stay retracted in their skeleton and they will not be able to feed.

Feeding: Tongues will eat small meaty foods provided by hand and will also benefit from additions of invertebrate foods and/or a D.S.B. setup.

Compatibility: They're nonaggressive and typically don't cause any trouble.

Placement: Tongues should be placed flat on the bottom, preferably on a soft substrate.

Reproduction/Propagation: Because of their form, they are not propagated, but *H. limax* has been known to reproduce on its own at times through the production of anthocauli. Broken off pieces of both have also been observed to recover and grow, but breaking these corals intentionally is not recommended.

Hardiness: They are often injured during collection or transport due to the presence of sharp septa, but they typically do very well once acclimated if they recover from any such injuries.

Pineapple Corals (also called Boulder, Brain, and Moon Corals)

Favia spp., *Montastraea* spp., and *Favites* spp.

Description: Pineapple corals are represented by a couple of genera and quite a few species, but they are all similar enough in appearance and care requirements that they can be lumped together. The majority of them are dome or boulder-shaped, but they may also be flattened or somewhat encrusting in form when

Part 4

living in deeper waters. While they are always attached to a hard substrate, they can be found in a variety of colors and patterns, but are most commonly found in various shades of green.

The colonies are made of round to polygonal polyps; each polyp is closely spaced and has a ring of hidden feeding tentacles that is kept under a flap/ring of tissue that surrounds its mouth. These will come out whenever food is detected.

To properly separate the species, you'll have to look at how the polyps are spaced relative to each other. Pineapple corals belonging to the genera *Favia* and *Montastraea* have distinct polyps (although they may be very close together), each of which have its own polyp margin and is typically more rounded in form. Those belonging to the genus *Favites*, on the other hand, have polyps with connected margins and take on more polygonal forms.

Lighting: Most pineapples will prefer moderate to high intensity lighting. However, they tend to be quite adaptable. As a very general rule, flat colonies that originated from dimmer areas can fare well in lower lighting.

Current: They prefer a moderate current and often will not expand if the flow is too strong.

Feeding: Pineapple corals will take small meaty foods if hand-fed and will also benefit from additions of invertebrate foods and/or a D.S.B. setup.

Compatibility: These are yet another type of coral that can develop long sweeper tentacles, despite the fact that they have very small feeding tentacles. They're there, though, and they can reach out a few inches at night, so be careful.

Placement: Other than needing room for the sweepers, they'll do fine just about anywhere that the current isn't too strong or too low.

Reproduction/Propagation: Due to their form, they are not propagated. However, they have been known to produce polyp buds.

Hardiness: Overall, they are very hardy corals, but they may suffer from recession, especially just after shipping. This is typically reversible as they become acclimated.

Part 4

Brain Corals (also called Maze Corals)

Platygyra spp. and *Oulophyllia* spp.

Description: These brain corals look like brains! Well, at least they're covered by meandering grooves that are similar to those that cover a brain. They are always attached to a hard substrate and are most commonly dome-shaped, but they may be encrusting as well. They are quite beautiful and come in a range of colors, including brown, green, pink, and gray. One thing you'll often see is a darker colored ridge with much lighter colored valleys between them. In fact, the valleys are oftentimes a fluorescent color, giving them a really neat appearance.

While it may not be obvious at first, all of the valleys are inhabited by little mouths and miniscule hidden feeding tentacles that will open up when food is present. Thus, once you spot them, there's really no feature that indicates where one polyp starts and another stops.

Lighting: Most brains will thrive under moderate to high intensity lighting. However, as a very general rule, flat colonies come from dimmer areas and thus can fare well in lower lighting.

Current: They prefer at least moderate flow but often will not expand if it is too strong.

Feeding: Brain corals will take small meaty foods if hand-fed and will also benefit from additions of invertebrate foods and/or a D.S.B. setup.

Compatibility: Here again is another type of coral that can produce long sweeper tentacles even though they have very short feeding tentacles. These can reach out several inches at night, so be careful.

Placement: Other than needing room for the sweepers, they'll do fine just about anywhere that the current isn't too strong or too low.

Reproduction/Propagation: Due to their form, they are not propagated.

Hardiness: Overall, they are very hardy corals; however, they may suffer from recession, especially just after shipping. This is typically reversible as they become acclimated to life in an aquarium.

Dented Brain Corals (also called Closed Brain Corals)

Symphyllia spp.

Description: Dented brains are found attached to hard substrates, and they are available in rounded, flat, or dome-like forms. They're typically fairly large and are covered by meandering grooves, like those of the "regular" brain coral Platygyra. However, they tend to have much larger ridges and wider valleys. They also come

Part 4

in several colors and patterns, which include red, brown, green, and cream, and they often have different colors in the valleys and on the ridges.

While you may not notice this upon first inspection, all of the valleys are inhabited by numerous mouths and small, hidden feeding tentacles that will open up when food is present. There aren't any features that indicate where one polyp starts and another stops, either.

Lighting: Dented brains can be found in a wide variety of environments and can thrive under moderate to high intensity lighting. However, they can also usually fare well under lower intensity lighting.

Current: They do well in a low to moderate current and won't fully expand their tissues if the current is too strong.

Feeding: Dented brains will take small meaty foods if hand-fed and will also benefit from additions of invertebrate foods and/or a D.S.B. setup.

Compatibility: Their feeding tentacles are very short and should not be a problem for other corals. As a result, they are quite nonaggressive and tend to be resistant to the stings of other corals.

Placement: Because they are nonaggressive and can tolerate a wide range of lighting intensities and currents, they can be placed just about anywhere in an aquarium.

Reproduction/Propagation: Due to their forms, most are not propagated.

Hardiness: They're consistently very hardy and are an excellent choice.

Flowerpot Corals (also called Daisy Corals)

Goniopora spp. and *Alveopora* spp.

Description: Flowerpots are some of the most beautiful corals you can find. Their skeletons can be round, domed, massive, or heavily branched, and they almost always live attached to a hard substrate, although at times they may be found free-living on soft bottoms. During the day, they'll extend polyps that look more like tentacles, which typically come in golden brown, green, or cream. These tentacle-like polyps do have their own "real" tentacles, though, which are sometimes a lighter color and can often reach a total length of up to 1 foot.

Figuring out what genera is what is easy, as all you have to do is count the number of tentacles on each of the long polyps. *Goniopora* will always have 24 tentacles per polyp, while *Alveopora* will always have only 12. It can be hard to get an exact count, but all you need to do is figure out if there are more than 12 or not.

Lighting: They can tolerate low to high intensity lighting, but they are unpredictable when it comes to what they prefer. Some hobbyists have had success only when placing them under low intensity illumination, while others seem to have success only after placing them under much brighter illumination. You may have to experiment a bit to see if you can find an area that suits a particular specimen best.

Current: Flowerpots will need a moderate current to thrive. If it's too low or too high, they won't expand well or at all. Turbulent flow is what will really make the polyps open up and reach out.

Feeding: Some *Goniopora* specimens will take very small meaty foods if hand-fed, but others will not, so you may have to experiment a little. *Alveopora* are even less likely to take anything you hand-feed them, but all flowerpots will require additions of invertebrate foods and/or a D.S.B. setup for long-term success.

Compatibility: The long, tentacle-like polyps can really reach out and touch their neighbors, and they have strong stings.

Placement: Due to the length of their polyps and strength of their stings, you'll need to give them plenty of room to expand while keeping them in an area with suitable current and lighting. Of the two, *Alveopora* specimens actually tend to have much shorter tentacles, so you can be a little less cautious with them if you want.

Reproduction/Propagation: If you look carefully to see where the skeleton is covered and possibly not covered in flesh, you may be able to break or saw off portions of branching colonies. Flowerpots are also known to produce polyp buds when doing well.

Hardiness: Sorry, but more bad news. Very, very few flowerpots make it through a year. It is very common for them to look great for up to several months and then begin to decline until they die, for no apparent reason. It is thought that this is because they need lots of food and cannot rely as much on their zooxanthellae, as the few success stories out there involve regular feedings and/or the use of D.S.B. setups to provide a steady supply of natural foods.

As I said, they'll look fine and may even seem to grow, but then the polyps often extend less and less, then tissue recession occurs, which is then followed by brown jelly infection and death. As is the case with the less than hardy elegance coral, the sad part is that flowerpots are still seen for sale everywhere despite their pathetic survival record. Do not be tempted, though, and keep in mind that if you don't plan on taking the time to care for one right and/or properly maintain a D.S.B. setup, YOU SHOULD NOT BUY ONE!

Turban Corals (also called Birdbath, Pagoda, and Scroll Corals)
Turbinaria spp.
Description: Tough one again. Members of this genus can take on a wide number of forms depending on the species, lighting, and current each is found in. They can range from massive, to columnar, to sheet-like, to cup-shaped, and more. They also vary in colors, which include tones of brown, gray, green, or olive and are all found attached to hard substrates. They also all have numerous slightly raised polyps that are connected by a thin layer of flesh covering the flat skeletal areas between them.

Those that live in shallower, brighter waters tend to have upright, more columnar forms that are covered on all surfaces by polyps. Conversely, those that come from deeper, dimmer waters tend to have flatter forms to collect more light and have

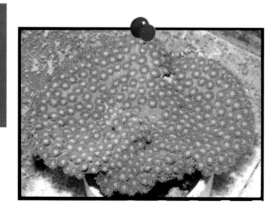

polyps only on their upper sides. In fact, one of the most common forms comes from such environments and has a form that resembles a birdbath (and is aptly called a "birdbath coral"), with a large, shallow, cup-shaped top on top of a pedestal with no polyps underneath. Overall, they are all very adaptable, and a single specimen may change growth forms many times to suit the conditions they are placed in.

Lighting: Turbans are exceptionally flexible when it comes to lighting and can do fine under just about anything. However, most will actually prefer lower lighting. Pay attention to their form more than any-thing else.

Current: They are also quite flexible when it comes to current, as long as it is strong enough to keep material from settling and collecting on them.

Feeding: Turbans will take small meaty foods if hand-fed and will also benefit from additions of invertebrate foods and/or a D.S.B. setup.

Compatibility: They don't cause trouble but may be injured by more aggressive corals.

Placement: They can be placed anywhere that currents will keep them clean and where they won't be victims of other coral aggression. Again, pay attention to their form and go from there.

Reproduction/Propagation: If healthy and thin enough, they can be fragmented by breaking or cutting them apart without too much worry. Sometimes the skeletons are so thick though that they are hard to deal with.

Hardiness: These are some of the most adaptable, hardiest corals around. I've seen them live when the rest of them quit.

Other Info: T. reniformis is a less commonly seen turban that is quite different in that is comes in thinner, often vertical, scroll-like sheets and is yellow to yellowish-green in color; it is thus typically called a "yellow scroll" coral. They will require moderate to strong illumination and a moderate to strong current. They are also far less hardy than other turbans, as they often suffer from fatal tissue recession.

Crystal Corals (also called Galaxy or Star Corals)

Galaxea astreata and Galaxea fascicularis

Description: Crystal corals have a unique look, as they have a skeleton with sort of a flat background dotted with raised corallites/polyps that have very large septa relative to their small size. If you look at the underside, you will see that the whole thing is actually a series of tubes that the polyps reside in, which are bound togeth-er by the background layers.

They are always found attached to hard substrates, and the overall form of colonies can vary from domed, to branched, to encrusting plates. Colonies may also come in various colors, including red, pink, brown, green, and gray, and the tentacles of each polyp are fairly short and often have lighter colored tips. Sometimes the ten-tacles may be rather clear, and when they are extended, they can obscure the entire skeletal background.

Lighting: Crystal corals will need moderate to high intensity lighting to thrive.

Part 4

Current: They do best with a low to moderate current.

Feeding: Crystal corals will take very small meaty foods if hand-fed and will also benefit from additions of invertebrate foods and/or a D.S.B. setup.

Compatibility: Aggressive. These corals are another wolf in sheep's clothing because they can produce very fine sweeper tentacles that may reach 1 foot in length at times. These are very powerful, very long, and are bad news for anything else around.

Placement: You have to be careful where you put them due to their long sweepers. Otherwise, they can thrive anywhere that the current and lighting are satisfactory. If anything, make sure to keep them out of high current areas, as they often respond by producing greater numbers of longer sweepers.

Reproduction/Propagation: They aren't propagated often due to their form, but they can be broken or cut up into chunks if you want to try. It really depends on the structure of each colony.

Hardiness: Larger colonies are often broken up during collection, and none of them seem to fare well during shipping. They are highly susceptible to brown jelly infections and RTN because of this. However, if they survive, they tend to be relatively hardy.

Other Info: They're just too aggressive relative to their size, so I don't think they're a good choice.

Acropora Corals (also called Staghorn, Table Top Corals, etc.)

Acropora spp.

Description: This is a tough one, as there are over 300 species of *Acropora*. They are small-polyped corals that are always attached to a hard substrate, forming branching colonies in a wide variety of forms. Some look like antlers and are appropriately called "staghorn" or "elkhorn" corals, others form tight clusters and are called "bush corals," while others form short-branched flat-topped colonies that are called "tabletops." There are really just too many to go over every form they can take. They also come in about every color of the rainbow you can think of, and sometimes the tips of the branches can be a different color than the rest of the colony. One characteristic unique to *Acropora* that you can easily spot is called a "terminal polyp," as every branch in an *Acropora* colony is tipped (terminated) by a single polyp. Most species of *Acropora* are sold in rather small clusters, or even single branches, but these can grow to nice-sized colonies relatively quickly compared to most other corals.

Lighting: Most *Acropora* will require moderate to high intensity lighting, with a preference for as much light as they can get. However, there are exceptions, as some can adapt to life under lower intensity lighting. I suggest you stick with high intensity for best results, though.

Current: There are many different forms that prefer different currents, but as a (very) general guideline, the closer-spaced their branches are, the stronger the current they'll need. Most will need very strong, turbulent flow to thrive.

Feeding: Some staghorn corals with relatively large polyps (they're still tiny) will eat very small meaty foods provided by hand, and all will benefit greatly from additions of invertebrate foods and/or a D.S.B. setup.

Compatibility: *Acropora* have small polyps and fine tentacles and can only be considered a problem if they actually grow very close to another coral that they can overtake. However, they are very susceptible to damage from other sorts of corals with longer and/or more potent tentacles.

Placement: *Acropora* can change their form and growth orientation in response to their placement. They should be able to thrive anywhere that they receive good lighting and strong, turbulent flow.

Reproduction/Propagation: *Acropora* are exceptionally easy to propagate, as they can be fragmented over and over.

Hardiness: *Acropora* can be very hardy if water quality is excellent and stable. However, if or when things go wrong, the whole colony is usually affected—and quickly.

Jewel Corals

Porites spp.
Description: Jewel corals are very small-polyped colonial corals that come in a wide variety of forms, from domed, to branched, to encrusting. They are also well known for their range of exceptional colors, which include vibrant red, pink, blue, and green, with others being brown or gray.

Lighting: They need moderate to high intensity lighting, with a preference for as much

Part 4

light as they can get. However, there are exceptions, as some can adapt to life under lower intensity lighting. I suggest you stick with high intensity for best results, though.

Current: Jewels prefer a strong current but will be okay with moderate currents.

Feeding: The polyps of a jewel coral are so small there really isn't anything you can feed them by hand. However, they will benefit greatly from additions of invertebrate foods and/or a D.S.B. setup.

Compatibility: Jewels have such small polyps/tentacles that they won't be a problem unless they actually grow into contact with another coral they may be able to overtake (rare). However, they are very susceptible to damage from other sorts of corals with longer and/or more potent tentacles.

Placement: They should be able to thrive anywhere that they receive good lighting and strong, turbulent flow.

Reproduction/Propagation: Jewels can be very easy to propagate if their form allows them to be fragmented.

Hardiness: They often ship very poorly, but can be fairly durable if they survive and become acclimated to aquarium life.

Other Info: Jewels can intentionally cover themselves with a mucous layer from time to time. This is normal, even when they are thriving, and it should be shed within a few days. However, if they stay enclosed in this wrapper for an extended period, it is likely a sign that the coral is unhappy with the environmental conditions.

Also, jewel corals are sometimes sold as domes that are perforated with "Christmas tree" worms *(Spirobranchus)*. These are often called "worm rocks" or something similar, although the "rock" is actually a living coral sold at a premium price. This association is quite natural, but people have a bad habit of thinking more of the beautifully colored worms than the coral and allow it to die. If you buy such a piece, worry about the requirements of the corals. If cared for correctly, you'll be more likely to keep the worms alive as well.

Bush Corals (also called Cauliflower or Cat's Paw Corals)
Pocillopora spp.
Description: Bush corals are small-polyped colonial corals that come in a very broad range of branched forms that are always attached to a hard substrate. Colonies can have numerous long and thin branches, fewer short and heavy branches, or any number of variations in between. They come in only a few colors, though they are most commonly brown or pink, and on occasion, green or blue.

These corals are well known for their "plasticity," which means that a single species can take on numerous forms. A species will change how it grows to whatever is best for the particular environment in which it lives. Thinner branches live in calmer waters, while heavier branches live in rougher waters, etc. Branch density also changes accordingly as well. Thus, it is essentially impossible to identify particular species by shape alone (as is the case with many other corals). Also, they can change as much as needed as they grow, allowing them to adapt to a change in flow when they are placed in aquariums, even if they are already large colonies.

Lighting: They need moderate to high intensity lighting and have a preference for as much light as they can get.

Current: There are many different forms of bush corals; they prefer different currents, but as a (very) general guideline, the heavier their branches are, the stronger the current they'll need. Most will prefer very strong, turbulent flow to thrive, but as mentioned, they can be very adaptive.

Feeding: The polyps of a bush coral are small, but you can still feed them very small meaty foods by hand. They will also benefit greatly from additions of invertebrate foods and/or a D.S.B. setup.

Compatibility: They have small polyps and fine tentacles, but they can also produce very small sweeper tentacles that are less than 1 inch long. As a result, they should only be considered a problem if they are very close to another coral. However, they are very susceptible to damage from other sorts of corals with longer and/or more potent tentacles.

Placement: They should be able to thrive anywhere that they receive good lighting and turbulent flow.

Reproduction/Propagation: They are exceptionally easy to propagate, as they can be fragmented over and over, and they have been known to reproduce sexually in aquariums by brooding and through polyp bailout.

Hardiness: Bush corals can be very hardy if water quality is excellent. However, they often tolerate shipping very poorly and suffer from RTN.

Bird's Nest Corals

Seriatopora hystrix
Description: Bird's nest corals are very small-polyped colonial corals that are found attached to hard substrates in branching forms. These forms have some variability, as there are typically more branches in shallow and/or clear waters and fewer in deeper/more turbid waters. However, these corals are easy to identify because their branches end in rather sharp points and the polyps lining them are arranged in neat, parallel rows. They come in few colors, including cream, brown, pink, or yellow.

Part 4

Lighting: They need moderate to high intensity lighting, with a preference for as much light as they can get.

Current: Bird's nests thrive in moderate, turbulent currents.

Feeding: The polyps of a bird's nest coral are so small there really isn't anything you can feed them by hand. However, they will benefit greatly from additions of invertebrate foods and/or a D.S.B. setup.

Compatibility: They have such small polyps/tentacles that they won't be a problem unless they actually grow into contact with another coral that they may be able to overtake. However, they are very susceptible to damage from other sorts of corals with longer and/or more potent tentacles.

Placement: They should be able to thrive anywhere that they receive good lighting and turbulent flow.

Reproduction/Propagation: They are exceptionally easy to propagate, as they can be fragmented over and over. They have also been known to reproduce on their own through polyp bailout.

Hardiness: Bird's nests are typically very hardy if water quality is excellent. However, they often tolerate shipping very poorly, have broken branches.

Cactus Corals

Pavona spp.
Description: Cactus corals come in a variety of forms depending on the species and the environmental conditions. They are always attached to hard substrates, but they may be encrusting to leafy or may even form heavy columns. Regardless of the overall form, they all have very unusual polyps that are often difficult to make out without a close inspection, and they also have very fine, pointy tentacles. They are almost always either brown or green.

Lighting: They prefer high intensity lighting but can typically do fine under lower intensity illumination.

Current: They need moderate to strong, turbulent currents to thrive.

Part 4

Feeding: Cactus corals have such unusual polyps that there really isn't anything you should feed them by hand. However, they will benefit greatly from additions of invertebrate foods and/or a D.S.B. setup.

Compatibility: They'll fool you. Even though they have tiny tentacles and recessed polyps, they can still produce sweeper tentacles up to a few inches long.

Placement: Be mindful of the sweepers, and make sure to give them plenty of light and current.

Reproduction/Propagation: They can be fragmented any way that their form allows.

Hardiness: They are typically very hardy if conditions are acceptable, and they are good choices as you give them sufficient room to send out sweepers and grow.

Cup Corals (also called Sun Corals)

Tubastrea **spp.**

Description: Now for something a bit different—Cup corals are nonsymbiotic. That is, they don't carry zooxanthellae and are not dependent on light. They are always attached to hard substrates and form fist-sized colonies of closely spaced, raised polyps. The common colorations are beautiful bright orange, sometimes with yellow polyps, completely orange or yellow, and/or white. However, there are a couple of species (T. micrantha and T. diaphana) that come in black, with dark-colored tentacles.

Lighting: Because they aren't symbiotic, they can thrive under any lighting conditions, from high intensity to complete darkness. A misconception used to be that they could be damaged by bright light because they weren't seen in bright areas around reefs, but this idea is false. Actually, they often cannot keep up with the growth rates of symbiotic corals and thus cannot compete with them for prime real estate. As a result, they typically aren't seen in areas where symbiotic corals are thriving.

Current: They can live in areas with a moderate current but prefer higher flow, which brings them a constant supply of food in the wild.

Feeding: Cup corals can't rely on

lighting to meet any part of their nutritional needs. Thus, they'll need to be fed small meaty foods regularly. They will also benefit greatly from additions of invertebrate foods and/or a D.S.B. setup.

Compatibility: They're docile corals with short tentacles and should not be considered a danger to other corals.

Placement: Cup corals are typically found upside down on overhangs and ledges. You don't have to do the same for them in an aquarium, though, as they can be placed just about anywhere that they won't be attacked or overrun by other aggressive or faster growing corals.

Reproduction/Propagation: They are not propagated due to their form. However, they will produce polyp buds.

Hardiness: Cup corals have proven to be very hardy, but only if given the attention they need. If fed regularly by some means, they suffer from few problems, if any.

Horn Corals

Hydnophora exesa and *Hydnophora rigida*
Description: Horn corals come in a range of forms, from encrusting, to massive, to branching, all of which are found attached to hard substrates. They are well-known for their bright, fluorescent green color. They are also unique in that they have odd knobs covering their skeletons called "hydophores," which are only found on corals of this genus. Aside from these small features (you'll have to look closely to notice them) and distinctive color, they typically look about the same as any other branching coral with small polyps, and the majority of the specimens offered for sale are branching varieties.

Lighting: Horns will thrive under strong illumination but will typically tolerate moderate intensity lighting.

Current: They need moderate to strong, turbulent flow to thrive.

Feeding: Horns will take small meaty foods if hand-fed and will also benefit from additions of invertebrate foods and/or a D.S.B. setup.

Compatibility: They can produce thin sweeper tentacles up to several inches long that carry a strong sting. They also readily produce mesenterial filaments and can damage just about any coral they come into contact with. For

Part 4

these reasons, they should be considered very aggressive.

Placement: Beware the sweeper tentacles, as they can be surprisingly long. If given enough room away from their neighbors, they should be able to thrive anywhere you put them as long as the lighting and current are acceptable.

Reproduction/Propagation: Horns are exceptionally easy to propagate because they can be fragmented over and over.

Hardiness: They may not ship well and often suffer from RTN and brown jelly infections, which cause the death of whole specimens. If they survive, they are typically able to adapt to aquarium life quite well. Once acclimatized, they can be relatively hardy if kept under optimal conditions.

Pipe Organ Corals
Tubipora musica

Description: Pipe organs are quite unique in that their skeletons are red in color. However, they are very different for less obvious reasons, too. While almost all of the other stony corals belong to the order Scleractinia, these belong to the order Alcyonacea, and are far more closely related to star polyps than to stony corals. Their rounded, massive colonial skeletons are always attached to hard substrates and are actually made of numerous hollow tubes joined by horizontal skeletal layers that hold them together. From these tubes emerge light-green, gray, or almost white polyps that look practically identical to those of clove or star polyps.

Lighting: Pipe organs need moderate to high intensity lighting and will not fare well under lower illumination.

Current: They need a low to moderate current and will not extend their polyps if the flow is too strong.

Feeding: Pipe organ corals will benefit from additions of invertebrate foods and/or a D.S.B. setup.

Compatibility: They have no tentacles like those of stony corals and should be considered nonaggressive. However, they may be damaged by nearby corals that have stinging tentacles.

Placement: As long as they are out of the range of any aggressive neighbors, they can be placed anywhere that lighting and current are satisfactory.

Reproduction/Propagation: The polyps are quite independent, so colonies can be broken or sawed apart, with only those polyps that may be damaged in the process being affected.

Hardiness: Some specimens seem to be the hardiest corals in an aquarium while others may slowly die for no apparent reason. They may have a greater dependence on food than typically thought, and may not receive enough in some aquariums.

Tips for Selecting Corals

Now that you've made it to this point, you should have a basic understanding of coral biology and a good idea of what it will take to successfully care for corals in general. Before you head to the store, however, you still need to finish reading this book and thinking about a few things. As the wheels start turning, don't forget that it is a bad idea to

Try to always pick corals that appear healthy in the aquarium shops.

It is important to learn basic signs of trouble. This coral has "bleached."

assume you can choose corals for your aquarium just because they are attractive and/or interesting. The information provided about each coral's hardiness, compatibility, lighting requirements, and other factors must all be given significant "weight" when making decisions. In addition, I think it's always a good idea to choose corals that can be easily propagated and spread around an aquarium.

Once you have an idea of what you want to do with your aquarium with respect to stocking, I suggest you make a written list of your "goals." Then, and only then, should you head for the store with the intent of buying instead of looking. Carrying your list with you and sticking to it will help prevent spontaneous purchases that may turn out to be problem purchases later. You should NEVER buy any coral that you have not researched and determined how it will fit into your plan. I know that's no fun and takes away some of the excitement of shopping. However, these aren't toys–they're living organisms that must be well taken care of or they'll die and/or kill something else.

What to Stay Away From

To help out as much as possible, I want to run through a few guidelines and specific things to watch for and avoid when shopping around for the specimens on your list. Following these suggestions and spending some time before buying can save you from worlds of aggravation later.

Don't buy any specimens that are damaged

You should always give a specimen a close inspection to check for any possible physical damage that may have occurred during collection and/or shipping. Always make sure to look at any areas where septa/skeletal structures are large, sharp, and/or protrude from the coral's body in particular, as these are the areas most likely to suffer from breakage, cuts, and abrasions. The most common problems that I see involve stony corals with broken septa that end up cutting right though the flesh that surrounds them.

Don't buy any specimens that will not expand

Most of the corals kept in aquariums will expand/polyp-out during the day and will close at night, although there are some that may stay expanded at all times. As a result, you'll need to watch out for corals that expand only partially or not at all. Corals that have been over-illuminated may not expand, as they may actually be poisoned by an overload of photosynthetic activity or burned by excessive exposure to UV light. They may also fail to expand if they are subjected to temperatures that are too high or too low, to poor water quality, or if the surrounding water currents are too strong or too weak. They may also come under attack by an aggressive, stinging neighbor or sickened by toxins given off by nearby corals.

Part 4

While most of these issues can be cleared up by making sure that environmental parameters are acceptable, or simply by moving a coral to a new spot, there's no reason for you to take unnecessary risks. This is why I suggest you let the store try to correct the problem by whatever means they can while you keep shopping.

Don't buy any specimens that have bleached

Under some conditions, like those that commonly cause corals to stay closed, many corals may also lose their color. Sometimes, when corals get too hot or too cold for a given amount of time or are subjected to rapid changes in lighting, they may turn completely white or even clear. This is called "coral bleaching" and occurs when a coral looses its zooxanthellae and pigments.

There are several possible and often interrelated causes; most corals don't recover and eventually starve to death. There are exceptions when corals become "reinfected" by zooxanthellae and do survive, but these are very uncommon in my experience. Thus, keep your eye out for corals that seem to be too pale in color or that are completely clear or white, and avoid them.

Don't buy any specimens that are artificially colored

Every once in a while you may come across a coral that is so brightly colored that it just doesn't look real, and the problem is that it might not be. Some dubious business folk have discovered that many corals will absorb dyes if they are soaked in them, with bright pink, magenta, and yellow being the colors of choice. This is sometimes done in an effort to mask a bleached coral so it can still be sold, but may also be performed on healthy corals, which are often sold at premium prices as "special" specimens.

Dyes have been shown to have deleterious effects on healthy corals, as they can interfere with light absorption by zooxanthellae, and they obviously aren't going to help bleached specimens that likely won't recover anyway. When corals do survive, it's only because the dye fades away over a period of a few days, leaving them as they were beforehand. It can be hard to decide if something has been dyed, as there are a few corals that are very brightly colored all by themselves. If you suspect a particular coral has been dyed, check up on the coral in question and see if it matches its typical description.

Don't buy any specimens that are suffering from "brown jelly" infection

If a coral is injured in some way, it may quickly become the victim of "brown jelly," a mass of bacteria and/or protozoa that attack an injured area and look something like globs of mucus. These microorganisms increase in numbers quickly, consume the flesh of the victim around the injury, and have a habit of spreading rapidly and destroying the rest of the coral, too, even if the jelly initially forms in an area with a seemingly minor injury.

Whole specimens are often killed in just a day or two and may be completely wiped out in as little as a few hours in extreme cases. To

Part 4

add to that, if an affected coral is subjected to strong currents, some of the jelly may blow away and travel to other corals, where it has the potential to come to rest and begin attacking them. I've been lucky enough to never have this happen in any of my own tanks. However, I have been unlucky enough to bring home more than one specimen that was completely overtaken by brown jelly in less than 24 hours. Thus, it is very important to avoid corals with even the smallest of physical injuries and especially those that already have jelly on them.

Don't buy any specimens that are suffering from "RTN"

Some specimens may also suffer from a condition commonly know as "rapid tissue necrosis," or "RTN." When it strikes, the tissues of a stony coral are simply sloughed away from the skeleton, leaving it completely clean and obviously dead. It can also spread very quickly and may completely wipe out a specimen in as little as a few hours in extreme cases. Unfortunately, once it starts, it typically doesn't stop. To date, no one has figured out exactly what causes it, and there are many ideas but none proven.

Luckily (if I can use that word), it usually affects only branching corals with small polyps. RTN almost always starts near the base of the colony and moves toward the tips of the branches. For this reason, look very closely (especially near the bases of these types of specimens) before making a purchase. If any of the white skeleton looks at all exposed, you should hold off and wait at least a day or two to see what happens.

Part 4

Don't buy any specimens that show receding tissues

Sometimes, if you look closely, you'll find that some stony corals seem to be peeling out of or off their skeletons, but not in the same way that you would see in a case of RTN. The flesh in this case doesn't seem to be sloughing off, dissolving, or turning to jelly, but it appears to have slowly moved back from the edge of the skeleton instead, leaving previously unexposed areas unprotected. This can be a reaction to stress, disease, or injury, but it is also common for established specimens, too, when calcium and alkalinity levels are too low and/or phosphate levels are too high. These less than favorable water quality conditions can prevent affected corals from forming new skeletal material and also cause them to lose their ability to stay attached to their already formed skeleton. Whatever the cause, it can still be fatal, so you need to look for and avoid it.

What you should watch for are corals that normally have an exposed or partially exposed skeletal base even when they are healthy, and take a look at the area where the flesh normally stops to see if it is still in place. Fortunately, this problem advances much more slowly than the others, and it is typically much more likely to be reversible if water quality problems are solved. However, you should still avoid purchasing a coral suffering from this condition.

Don't buy any specimens that are known to have poor survival rates

The list will change depending on whom you ask, but here are a few corals that are best known for dying in aquariums. As always,

Part 4

there are exceptions, as some of these may be tough as nails in someone's tank, but these are indeed exceptions. The problem is that many will do just fine for weeks, months, or maybe even a year and then slowly fade away until dead, letting you believe everything is great for quite a while.

As far as stony corals go, the elegance coral, torch coral, flowerpot coral (all species), and yellow scroll coral should all be left alone, as there are plenty of other hardier things to choose from. In my own experience, "worm rock" pieces of the otherwise hardy jewel coral should be avoided as well, because the worms almost always die, after which the coral many times follows.

Cup corals and other nonsymbiotic specimens are best avoided, too. Many cups themselves have proven to be quite hardy when fed regularly, but a few, particularly *Tubastrea micranthus*, just won't make it no matter what you try. The same goes for some tree leathers, like *Nepthea* sp., the nonphotosynthetic varieties of gorgonians, and the carnation corals, which belong to the genus *Dendronephthya*. Speaking of carnations, people have finally caught on that they won't live, and you hardly ever see them. However, some other specimens are still everywhere you look, so don't be fooled by their presence into thinking that availability has anything in the world to do with hardiness.

The End

Organizations

Federation of American Aquarium Societies (FAAS)

Secretary: Jane Benes
E-mail: Jbenes01@yahoo.com
www.gcca.net/faas

Federation of British Aquatic Societies (FBAS)

Secretary: Vivienne Pearce
E-mail: Webmaster@fbas.co.uk
www.fbas.co.uk

International Marinelife Alliance (IMA)

President: Vaughan R. Pratt
E-mail: info@ma
rine.org
www.marine.org

Marine Aquarium Council (MAC)

923 Nu'uanu Avenue
Honolulu, HI 96817
Telephone: (808) 550-8217
Fax: (808) 550-8317
E-mail: info@aquariumcouncil.org
www.aquariumcouncil.org

Marine Aquarium Societies of North America (MASNA)

Director of Membership/Secretary: Cheri
Phillips
E-mail: cheri@uniquesensations.com
www.masna.org

ReefGuardian International

2829 Bird Avenue-Suite 5
PMB 162
Miami, FL 33133-4668
E-mail: info@ReefGuardian.org
www.reefguardian.org

The Coral Reef Alliance

417 Montgomery Street, Suite 205
San Francisco, CA 94104
Telephone: (888) CORAL-REEF
Fax: (415) 834-0999
E-mail: info@coral.org
www.coralreefalliance.org

The International Federation of Online Clubs and Aquatic Societies (IFOCAS)

E-mail: ifocas@ifocas.fsworld.co.uk
www.ifocas.fsworld.co.uk

Publications

Tropical Fish Hobbyist Magazine

T.F.H. Publications, Inc.

1 TFH Plaza

Third and Union Avenues

Neptune City, NJ 07753

Telephone: (800) 631-2188

E-mail: info@tfh.com

www.tfh.com

Internet Resources

AquaLink

(www.aqualink.com)

The largest aquaria web resource in the world, AquaLink provides fishkeepers with information on a variety of topics, including freshwater and marine fish, aquatic plants, goldfish, reef systems, invertebrates, and corals.

Aquaria Central

(www.aquariacentral.com)

Aquaria Central is an online resource offering species profiles, help forums, chat rooms, and a variety of aquaria articles. To date, there are more than 700 species profiles listed on this website's searchable database.

AquariumHobbyist

(www.aquariumhobbyist.com)

This website lists upcoming marine-related events, as well as commercial pages, chat rooms, news, a classifieds section, and care information.

Reef Central

(www.reefcentral.com)

Reef Central is an online community that shares information regarding the marine and reef aquarium hobby. The site includes access to discussion forums, photo galleries, chat rooms, and news.

Reefs.Org

(www.reefs.org)

An online interactive community, Reefs.Org is home to an active bulletin board, reference library, chat room, monthly periodical, and online curriculum.

Wet Web Media

(www.wetwebmedia.com)

This website features extensive aquarium, fish, and aquatic information, with numerous articles on marine aquariums, freshwater aquariums, aquarium plants, ponds, and other related topics.

Index to Scientific Names

A

Acropora spp., 120-121
Actinodiscus, 81
Alcyonium spp., 90-92
Alveopora spp., 116-118, 130
Amplexidiscus fenestrafer, 82
Anthelia spp., 84-85

B

Briareum asbestinium, 97-98
Briareum stechei, 97-98

C

Capnella spp., 92-93
Catalaphyllia jardinei, 104-105
Caulastrea echinulata, 112-113
Caulastrea furcata, 112-113
Cladiella spp., 90-92
Clavularia spp., 89-90
Clavularia viridis, 88
Cynaria lacrymalis, 102-103

D

Dendronephthya spp., 136
Discosoma spp., 80-81

E

Eunicea spp., 95
Euphyllia ancora, 109-110
Euphyllia divisa, 110-111
Euphyllia glabrescens, 111-112
Euphyllia paradivisa, 110-111
Euphyllia parancora, 109-110

F

Favia spp., 113-114
Favites spp., 113-114
Fungia spp., 100-101

G

Galaxea astreata, 119-120
Galaxea fascicularis, 119-120
Goniopora spp., 116-118
Gorgonia spp., 96

H

Heliofungia actiniformis, 101
Herpolitha limax, 113
Hydnophora exesa, 126-127
Hydnophora rigida, 126-127

Index

A

Acetates, 32

Actinic blue lighting, 53

Activated carbon, 32

Alkalinity, 47-48, 135

Ammonia, 47

Anchor corals, 109-110

Anthocauli, 39-40

Anthozoa, 14

Aragonite, 16-17, 23, 48, 58, 76

Arthropoda, 12

Asexual reproduction, 35, 37-40

Auto-fragmentation, 38, 40

B

Bilateral symmetry, 13

Biological filtration, 47

Bird's nest corals, 123-124

Brain corals, 11, 19, 22, 39, 71, 103-104, 114-115

    Closed, 115-116

    Dented, 116

    lobo, 106-107

    Maze, 114-115

    Moon, 113-114

    Open, 103-104

    Pineapple, 113-114

Branch dropping, 38

Brine shrimp, 56

Bubble corals, 107-109

Bull's-eye mushrooms, 81-82

Bush corals, 122-123

Button polyps, 57, 64

C

Cabbage leather corals, 93-94

Cactus corals, 124-125

Calcium carbonate, 16

Calcium reactor, 48

Calcium, 16, 47-48, 79, 135

Candy cane corals, 112

Carbon dioxide, 16, 23

Carnation corals, 136

Circulation, 48-49

Closed brain corals, 115-116

Clove polyps, 84, 89-90

Cnidarians, 11-14

Cnidocytes, 14, 28-30

Colonial anemones, 85-87

Colonial polyps, 13, 21, 64

Colt corals, 90-91